Reawakening the Learner

Creating Learner-Centric, Standards-Driven Schools

Copper Stoll and Gene Giddings

D1531220

ROWMAN & LITTLEFIELD EDUCATION

A division of
ROWMAN & LITTLEFIELD PUBLISHERS, INC.
Lanham • New York • Toronto • Plymouth, UK

Published by Rowman & Littlefield Education
A division of Rowman & Littlefield Publishers, Inc.
A wholly owned subsidary of The Rowman & Littlefield Publishing Group, Inc.
4501 Forbes Boulevard, Suite 200, Lanham, Maryland 20706
www.rowman.com

10 Thornbury Road, Plymouth PL6 7PP, United Kingdom

Copyright © 2012 by Copper Stoll and Gene Giddings

All rights reserved. No part of this book may be reproduced in any form or by any electronic or mechanical means, including information storage and retrieval systems, without written permission from the publisher, except by a reviewer who may quote passages in a review.

British Library Cataloguing in Publication Information Available

Library of Congress Cataloging-in-Publication Data

Stoll, Copper, 1957–
  Reawakening the learner : creating learner-centric, standards-driven schools /
Copper Stoll and Gene Giddings.
      p. cm.
  Includes bibliographical references.
  ISBN 978-1-61048-696-5 (cloth : alk. paper) — ISBN 978-1-61048-697-2 (pbk. : alk.
paper) — ISBN 978-1-61048-698-9 (ebook)
  1. School improvement programs—United States. 2. Student-centered learning—United
States. 3. Education—Standards—United States. I. Giddings, Gene, 1951– II. Title.
  LB2822.82.S84185 2012
  371.2'07—dc23   2012006768

♾™ The paper used in this publication meets the minimum requirements of
American National Standard for Information Sciences—Permanence of Paper
for Printed Library Materials, ANSI/NISO Z39.48-1992.

Printed in the United States of America

371.207
S875r

Contents

Section 4:
The Learner Improvement Cycle
87

Section 5:
Wide Awake in the Twenty-First Century:
Proficiency for All
167

Foreword

This book is about fundamental and foundational change in the way schools are run. The magnitude of the change suggested by Copper Stoll and Gene Giddings is captured in their title. They explain that learners in our current system are sleepwalking through their educational opportunities due to the fact that they haven't been woken up by their teachers and become active partners in their learning. The picture the authors provide for the future of education is nothing less than a paradigm shift. However, it is a shift that is currently being enacted in Adams County School District 50 in Colorado, whose story forms the basis for the authors' recommendations.

"The reawakening" as described by Stoll and Giddings involves three steps, or three necessary behaviors, in which districts must engage: (1) defining a common moral purpose, (2) creating a culture that supports change, and (3) committing to the Learner Improvement Cycle. The authors explain that developing a common moral purpose becomes the foundation upon which all stakeholders, including the learners, must agree in order to ensure a common direction. The development of readiness for change, a trust-to-doubt process, and collective efficacy for learners, teachers, principals, and the community is the culture for change and continuous improvement. The components of the Learner Improvement Cycle (assessment, evaluation, planning, and learning) establish an educational environment that require learners to be active participants.

The authors not only provide clear guidelines regarding how a district might address their triad of behaviors, but also provide illustrations of how these behaviors manifest in the real world by using stories from the principals, teachers, learners, and parents in Adams County School District 50 who are living the reawakening process.

Not surprisingly, a common moral purpose is the initial and foundational step. Specifically, Stoll and Giddings contend that all stakeholders must reach a consensus that a truly equitable system of education must ensure that all learners reach proficiency. A culture that supports this purpose requires a trust-to-doubt orientation. This orientation engenders a system in which all stakeholders, including learners, are able to tell each other when the common moral purpose is not being upheld. Staff is able to doubt current practices and suggest ways to improve. At an operational level, the Learner Improvement Cycle provides the structure for day-to-day life. Central to this cycle is learner involvement in the assessment as learning process. This goes well beyond mere distinctions between formative and summative assessments. Rather, it involves creating an assessment system where learners are motivated to be assessed so that they might "show what they know."

When taken to heart, the recommendations made in *Reawakening the Learner* will drastically and permanently change the business of schooling in this country. In keeping with this sobering fact, the authors call for a national dialogue of educational experts to reinvent public education in such a way that all students are engaged as learners and are given enough time and support to reach proficiency in all standards. Those who read *Reawakening the Learner* will most probably never think of schooling in the same way as they did prior to opening its cover.

Robert J. Marzano, PhD
December 2010

Acknowledgments

Special thanks go to our spouses, Dave and Sue, who provided the loving support, the time, and the independence to do this work. And to our children, Vanessa Giddings Fisher, Jason Fisher, Genevieve Travis, Justin Travis, Randy Stoll, Kristen Stoll, Ryan Stoll, Brea Burgie Christopherson, Dan Burgie Christopherson, Brent Burgie, friends, and family, thank you for your encouragement and cheerleading along the way.

Thank you to the following groups for their feedback during the spring of 2008 as we were developing the concepts for the book: Barb Kerin; Regis 8w1 spring 08 Philosophy of Education class; D50 MS principals; DU Principal preparation program students; EDFD 600 Spring 8w2 Philosophy of Ed class on learner-centered component.

Thank you to these people who took time to read and provide feedback and challenge our thinking: Jessie Case, mother of Copper Stoll; Annette Sulzman, retired Executive Director of Quality Improvement, Douglas County; Katheryn Keyes and Renee Bauer, Adams County School District 50 Standards-Based Systems coaches; Heidi Patton, Adams County School District 50 Language Arts teacher; Roberta Selleck, Superintendent of Adams County School District 50; Rich Delorenzo, ReInventing Schools Coalition; and Bob Marzano from Marzano Research Laboratories.

A special thanks to BJ Pell, Steve Peterson, and Jessie Case who provided tranquil places for us to write and reflect; and the staff at the Cottonwood Hot Springs and Spa, Buena Vista, Colorado, and La Quinta Inn, Westminster, Colorado, who also provided venues for our creativity.

CREDITS

Credit: Source: From *The Art and Science of Teaching: A Comprehensive Framework for Effective Instruction* (p. 21), by Robert J. Marzano, Alexandria, VA: ASCD. © 2007 by ASCD. Reprinted with permission. Learn more about ASCD at www.ascd.org.

Credit: Source: From *Better Learning through Structured Teaching: A Framework for the Gradual Release of Responsibility* (p. 44), by Douglas Fischer and Nancy Frey, Alexandria, VA: ASCD. © 2008 by ASCD. Reprinted with permission. Learn more about ASCD at www.ascd.org.

Reproduced with permission of Harvard Business Publishing from *Leading Change* by John Kotter, HBS Press, 1996.

Section 1

PUBLIC EDUCATION: YESTERDAY'S ANSWERS TO TWENTY-FIRST-CENTURY NEEDS

We must learn to reawaken and keep ourselves awake, not by mechanical aid, but by an infinite expectation of the dawn.

—Henry David Thoreau

Overarching, Essential Question for
Reawakening the Learner: Creating Learner-Centered, Standards-Driven Schools

How does our society create schools to ensure *proficiency for all* learners to meet the ever-changing needs of the twenty-first century?

The Problem: Schools Are Not Structured to Prepare Learners for the Twenty-First Century

Fundamental components of chapter 1:

- One District's Story
- Increased Expectations and Accountability
- Creating Twenty-First Century Citizens
- Vision for the Twenty-First Century
- Structure of the Book
- Essential Question and Enduring Understandings
- Key Points in Chapter 1

Guiding Questions for Chapter 1:

1. Does the data indicate that the current structure of public education will prepare America's children for twenty-first-century needs?
2. How has the purpose of public education changed over time?
3. What skills and knowledge will learners need to be successful in the twenty-first century?
4. What resources and structures need to be included as society redesigns public education?

ONE DISTRICT'S STORY

Adams County School District 50, a suburban district in Colorado with urban issues, is witnessing a time of drastically changing demographics, becoming a Hispanic majority district in the 2003–2004 school year to its current proportion of 69 percent in 2010. This district is typical of many districts where there is declining enrollment (from 11,231 in 2000 to 9,862 in 2010) due to white flight, aging neighborhoods, tougher immigration laws, and open enrollment for other educational options. There is also an increase in the number of students who live in poverty (40 percent in 2000 to 75 percent in 2010), many of whom are second-language learners (20 percent in 2000 to 43 percent in 2010).

The district had employed programs to raise achievement, changed teaching practices, and to its credit has kept its achievement scores mostly stable during this drastic time of change. In spite of its best efforts, the district has low graduation rates that hover around 66 percent, significant numbers of students requiring remediation in college, and was placed on "academic watch" by the Colorado Department of Education in fall 2007. Increasing demands of No Child Left Behind (NCLB) have caused the district to fall farther behind in making Adequate Yearly Progress (AYP), mostly in the subgroups of special education and English-Language Learners (ELL). The district's staff was looking for the "silver bullet" to increase achievement, when what they needed was an entire systems overhaul.

District Achievement Data

The aggregated state achievement scores for Adams County School District 50 for the 2006–2010 school years on the Colorado Student Assessment Program (CSAP) showed less than 50 percent of elementary-school students scoring consistently at the proficient and advanced levels in math and reading, and less than 30 percent scoring proficient and advanced in writing. Twenty to 30 percent of middle-school students scored proficient or advanced in math, approximately 40 percent in reading, while in the 30 percent did so in writing. High-school students scored in the tens and single digits in math, forties in reading and mid to high twenties in writing.

Colorado State Achievement Results

District 50 is one of the seven lowest-performing districts in the state of Colorado. Although the State of Colorado has been a standard-referenced state since 1993, at best only two-thirds of the state's students are scoring at or above proficiency in fifth-, eighth-, and tenth-grade reading and fifth-grade math. While eighth- and tenth-grade math results show student improvement, still only half to a third are proficient or advanced, respectively. Current practices find learners being taught in teacher-directed classrooms being passively or ritualistically engaged. In analyzing the results of state achievement since its inception, there have been small increments of growth.

National Assessment of Educational Progress (NAEP) Results

In analyzing the achievement results on a national scale, similar minimal growth is exhibited. Using the results of the 2005 and 2009 National Assessment of Educational Progress (NAEP), zero to six scaled points of growth in math and reading (using a scaled score) are shown nationally. In disaggregating the results by state, Colorado shows relatively one to six scaled score point growth for the same years.

These results indicate the ineffectiveness of the current system of public education. Is the current system capable of increasing student learning? Can strategies and structures, used for the past one hundred years, support the increasing expectations in the twenty-first century?

INCREASED EXPECTATIONS AND ACCOUNTABILITY

Expecting all Learners to Be Proficient

The goal of public education has changed, but the structure for education has not. Public education has transformed from an educational system at the turn of the nineteenth century that provided education for some; to one in the early twentieth century that required education for all (mandatory attendance); in the late twentieth century, afforded proficiency for some; and now in the early twenty-first century, the expectation is *proficiency for all* (Lezotte 1997).

All states have had a mandatory student attendance law for some part of the last ninety years (1918–2008) (Sass 2008), but now there's an expectation of *proficiency for all*. Does the United States have a school system that can accomplish *proficiency for all* children, even those who have special needs, live in poverty, and/or learn English as a second language?

Increased Accountability: Meeting NCLB Requirements

There is rising frustration among educators because they have not been able to get improved student results within the current structure of the American public-school system. This is evidenced by district, state, and national plateauing or minimal growth in standardized test scores.

Schools today must meet two goals: (1) prepare students for the twenty-first century (Partnership for 21st Century Skills 2008) and (2) "close the achievement gap with accountability, flexibility and choice so no child is left behind" (PL 107-110 The No Child Left Behind Act 2001). The goal of NCLB (2001) has caused us to look at disaggregated groups, which has placed added focus on children with special needs and who live in poverty. In the current school structure, the label these students carry results in excuse-making for their lack of proficiency attainment. NCLB states all children must be proficient; so it is necessary to look at the current foundations and structures that are in place. The determination must be made if the goals can be reached; if not, the system must be reinvented.

There is a discrepancy between current skills and knowledge taught to our students and what is needed to be competitive in the twenty-first century. Data indicates schools have made negligible progress toward the goal of 100 percent proficiency in reading and math by 2014, as defined by each state and approved by the US Department of Education, outlined by NCLB. Students, learning in the current system, are not proficient in the basic skills to-date. What chance do students have to be ready with the skills and knowledge necessary for the twenty-first century to adapt to an ever-changing economic global reality?

The authors' contention is that the current institution's: (a) time-based agrarian calendar, (b) factory-like grade levels, and (c) rote learning for standardized tests won't get the desired results. Educational practice must be challenged if it is not helping students achieve their objectives and meet the mission of public education, *proficiency for all* (NCLB's requirement). Challenging the nineteenth-century agrarian calendar and a twentieth-century factory (grade-level, age-based) model is just a beginning.

So, what is needed in a school system to create citizens ready to meet the challenges of the twenty-first century?

CREATING TWENTY-FIRST CENTURY CITIZENS

Figure 1.1 shows the foundational educational system inputs needed to create twenty-first-century educators and citizens (Partnership for 21st Century Skills 2008).

The elements described in this section are the skills, knowledge, and expertise students must master to succeed in work and life in the twenty-first century. The system inputs (standards and assessments, professional development, curriculum and instruction, and learning environments) are the educational structures needed to make these twenty-first-century skills and knowledge become a reality.

VISION FOR THE TWENTY-FIRST CENTURY

The following are a list of suggested skills and knowledge, from the Partnership for the 21st Century (2008):

Twenty-First Century Content and Skills

1. Mastery of the traditional core subjects is still essential for students in the twenty-first century: (a) language arts, (b) mathematics, (c) science, (d) social sciences, (e) world languages, and (f) the arts. The Partnership for 21st Century (2008) advocates the integration of twenty-first-century themes: (a) global awareness, (b) financial, economic, business, and entrepreneurial literacy, (c) civic literacy, and (d) health literacy into the core curriculum.
2. The process skills needed to add relevance and rigor to the core and twenty-first century content are: (a) creativity, (b) problem solving and (c) collaboration.
3. New literacy skills for the twenty-first century include: (a) information literacy, (b) media literacy, and (c) the acquisition of technology skills.
4. As a citizen of the twenty-first century, learners will need to exhibit life-skill traits of: (a) adaptability, (b) initiative, (c) persistence, (d) accountability, (e) cultural proficiency, (f) active citizenry, and (g) responsibility.

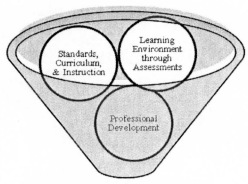

Figure 1.1.
The Twenty-First Century Citizen

21st Century Citizen

Core and 21st Century content   Creativity

Problem Solving   Collaboration

New Literacy Skills   Skills for Life

Twenty-First Century Support Systems

The critical systems necessary to ensure student mastery of twenty-first century skills are twenty-first century: (a) standards, (b) assessments, (c) curriculum, (d) instruction, (e) professional development, and (f) learning environments. These must be aligned to produce a support system that produces twenty-first-century outcomes for today's students (Partnership for the 21st Century 2008).

The Discrepancy between the Twenty-First-Century Vision and Our Current Reality

A public-school system must be created that removes the constraints of past educational practices that are not conducive to *proficiency for all* and twenty-first-century skill and knowledge acquisition. This new system requires *performance* of skills, knowledge, and attitudes to prepare students for jobs that have not yet been created (Pink 2006). Students need the time and support to master the standards of academic foundational skills and knowledge, as well as character skills of adaptability, persistence, and initiative.

Creating twenty-first-century educators is paramount in preparing learners for the twenty-first century. Most teachers weren't taught these skills or content in their own K–12 schooling, nor were they taught how to teach students in this manner in their preservice training. Most teachers were taught how to teach middle-class, English-speaking students, and aren't equipped to address needs of changing demographics in America. Teachers must be retrained for their roles in the twenty-first century. If independent-thinking citizens are to be ready for the changing world they will inherit, teachers will need to learn how to leverage students to play an active role in their own education, instead of reinforcing passive and compliant learners who are dependent on the teacher.

Table 1.1 highlights the discrepancies between the current practice and the practice needed to create twenty-first-century citizens.

Table 1.1.　Gap Analysis on Twenty-First-Century Citizen Outcomes

Areas for Change	Current Practices	Practices Needed to Create Twenty-First-Century Citizens
Core and twenty-first-century content	Core content: language arts, math, science, social sciences, world languages, the arts	Add twenty-first-century themes of global awareness, financial, civic, and health literacy
Creativity, problem-solving, and collaboration	Dependent on the teacher's knowledge and interest	Embedded and measured in the curriculum
Information, media literacy, and technology skills	Dependent on availability of technology resources; the teacher's knowledge and interest	Embedded and measured in the curriculum
New life skills: adaptability, initiative, persistence, accountability, cultural proficiency, active citizenry, and responsibility	Not measured; intermittently taught	Embedded and measured in the curriculum

With a *proficiency for all* focus, students need to be involved in their own education; the goal of *proficiency for all* can't be reached without them. What is needed for students is: (a) more relevance, (b) more ownership of learning, and (c) more emphasis on critical-thinking skills with less accumulation of discrete knowledge. Teachers and staff are working as hard as they know how. The students are the untapped resource. See Table 1.2.

Our society has gained all it can out of a system that was designed to meet the needs of the late nineteenth and twentieth centuries. Schools need to be restructured to meet the needs of the twenty-first century and the new student population.

Table 1.2. Gap Analysis for Foundational Educational System Inputs

Areas to Change	Current Practices	Changes Needed for the Educational Structure to Create Twenty-First-Century Citizens
Standards/Curriculum	Too many standards to master in time allocated; considers textbook or program as the curriculum	Identifies standards that comprise a guaranteed viable curriculum (GVC); students understand the GVC; ensures GVC is learned
Assessing	Used to rank and sort students	Inform instruction; students are partners in the creation
Evaluating	The evaluation of assessments are not used to inform instruction	Evaluate assessments with the student to determine strengths and next learning
Planning	Teacher-directed planning often time-based on scope and sequence of textbook	Involves students to write and monitor goals
Learning	Teacher-directed; learners learn at the same pace; teaches to the middle of the class	Learner-centered; differentiates and paces for each learner; balances the kind of instruction to ensure learning
Professional Development	Site-based: based on programs, textbook adoption or latest fad Drive-by model	Based on systemic student needs, differentiated for teacher capacity; systemic capacity building over time
Learning Environment	Teacher-centered content and code of conduct; not transparent; only student-to-teacher interactions	Learner-centered: partner in shared vision of the classroom; time is the variable for each student; student-to-student and student-to-teacher interactions; transparent processes

STRUCTURE OF THE BOOK

The authors' purpose for writing this book is to provide evidence that the current system of education is not working for all students and propose a new structure to create the kind of schools our children deserve in order to be proficient and productive citizens in the twenty-first century. It will take a national moral purpose of creating systems that blend the educational philosophies to provide *proficiency for all*. This requires breaking the current system and the creation of "schooling" that is fundamentally different than our current school system. This book focuses primarily on creating the conditions for students to reawaken into interdependent learners in the twenty-first century.

It has become obvious that schools need to create and leverage consensus among the staff members' individual values in order to forge a *common moral purpose*. A compliance mentality, prevalent in so many school systems, never gets stakeholders to a *common moral purpose*. Some schools *demand* compliance but never capture the hearts and souls of those doing the work. In education, the principles of *readiness for change*, *trust-to-doubt*, and *collective efficacy* prepare the school culture for a radical change.

The final lever is magnifying the focus on the Learner Improvement Cycle. The interdependence of all aspects of the Learner Improvement Cycle requires that the cycle be implemented as a set: (a) *assessing*, (b) *evaluating*, (c) *planning*, and *(d) learning*. Improvement of one aspect of the Learner Improvement Cycle cannot be accomplished without impacting the others; it is necessary to improve them all together.

Using a Continuum with Evidence to Plan Progress

Using the structure of continua assists in describing the developmental process in which teachers and the *principalship* must progress to reach a learner-centric, standards-driven environment. The term *principalship* is used to describe the administration and teacher leadership who guide the growth of a school. The continua are intentionally open in order to posit ideas and processes but not mandate a product or a solution.

School improvement is a process that every school must journey itself. The authors intend the continua to be a guide for school stakeholders to use in reawakening their learners. Continua have been developed in order to describe the journey of teachers and the principalship toward blending essentialism and progressivism into an essential-progressivist philosophy. Essential-progressivism will be explored in chapter 2.

The authors intend that stakeholders will self-evaluate their status and set goals to progress along each continuum. The principalship can use the continua to assess the school's placement on the continua and visualize the path to lead their school's culture to the next step. This may mean that principals and teacher leaders have to increase and improve their own skill and knowledge set prior to being able to move their staff forward.

It is the authors' intent that the continua guide the structure of the book. Each continuum consists of four developmental stages:

> In the *Beginning* stage, the assumption is the staff is unwilling or unable to perform the necessary tasks. They either don't know how to change current practice or they are unwilling to confront the brutal facts (Schmoker 2006) of their situation and change the conditions.
>
> During the *Developing* phase, staff is beginning to develop the prerequisite skills for the desired outcome and engage in professional development, which ensures each staff member has a common set of skills and knowledge.
>
> In the *Proficient* category, staff must have the skills and be able to apply them in learner-centric and standards-driven ways. In the classroom, the teacher is creating the conditions for students to partner with other students and their teacher. In the school, students become actively involved in providing input for the vision and the procedures for the school.
>
> At the *Advanced* level, students assume responsibility for the sustainability of the concept, and are actively involved in creating solutions to real-world problems and making relevant real-life connections, which are evaluated on a public standard.

These four components: beginning, developing, proficient, and advanced, provide insights into the development of a learner-centric, standards-driven system. The intent is for stakeholders, as a whole, to evaluate their place on the continua and to intentionally plan to make progress toward proficient or advanced behaviors.

Continuous Improvement

Embedded in each continuum is a Plan-Do-Check-Adjust (PDCA) continuous improvement cycle. This systemic thinking is necessary to design, implement, monitor, and fine-tune each component of the reform model. In order to develop each component of *Reawakening the Learner*, it is necessary for the principalship to create a plan to guide the process. This must include a *plan* phase in which a staff must create a process. This involves the discovery of root causes, and looks for leverage points in the system to improve results. Stakeholders can engage in readings and discussions. Key Performance Indicators (KPIs) must be defined to measure progress. During the *do* phase, each stakeholder group is responsible for carrying out and supporting the plan. The *check* phase involves assessments of KPIs from self, peers, supervisors, parents, and students to determine if the stakeholders' actions produce the desired results. The *adjust* phase then supports the stakeholders refining goals and action plans to better align actions with outcomes.

At the end of the teacher continua in the Learner Improvement Cycle is a suggested list of evidences that document progress: (a) artifacts; (b) agendas of meetings; (c) Specific, Measureable, Attainable, Results-oriented, Time-bound, Evaluate, Reviewed (SMARTER) goals (DuFour and Eaker 1998; Shaun n.d.); (d) survey results; (e) anecdotal comments; (f) calendars; (g) matrices; (h) data rosters; (i) evidence of communication; (j) professional development; and (k) evidence of celebrations (Eaker, DuFour, and Burnette 2002). The *suggested evidence* of proficient or better practices provides a menu of key performance indicators that provide stakeholders a gauge of learner-centric, standards-based practices.

District 50 is used as a case study to share firsthand accounts of these practices in action. Conversations with the stakeholders will bring these ideas to life. Questions and answers for the principal, teachers, learners, and parents are captured after the continua. Readers can use the interview questions posed as a preassessment of the practice in the reader's school to place themselves on the continua as baseline data. The readers can then begin developing a plan to move themselves toward the *advanced* level.

ESSENTIAL QUESTION AND ENDURING UNDERSTANDINGS

Public education has the standards, the dedicated staff, and the goal of reaching *proficiency for all*. What untapped resources are available to meet this goal? The students! That's who's been "napping" in public education all these years. Public education needs to reawaken the students to make them partners in their education, instead of thinking of them as the product.

Wiggins and McTighe (2005) purport that in any learning experience, the learning should center on essential questions and enduring understandings. Essential questions provide a scaffold for the learning as it occurs. The essential question of this book is:

> How does our society create schools to ensure *proficiency for all* learners to meet the ever-changing needs in the twenty-first century?

In this book, the case is built through guiding questions and key points to bring life to these enduring understandings:

> Schools must be restructured to satisfy the new expectations of *proficiency for all* students.

Capacity must be built in principals, teachers, and students to partner in achieving *proficiency for all.*

The system will sustain and improve practice by using a continuous improvement cycle.

In chapter 1, evidence was presented that the current system is not meeting the needs of the learners in our school systems. Twenty-first-century learners must be educated in a twenty-first-century system with twenty-first-century educators in order for *all* to be proficient. In the next chapter, a system is proposed that can mitigate many of the discrepancies between the current system and what will be needed. The major components for the proposed model are synthesized from major theorists in each field. These components will be explained in chapter 2 and then detailed in chapters 3–10.

Key Points in Chapter 1:

1. Does the data indicate that the current structure of public education will prepare children for twenty-first-century needs?
   No, the current data from local, state, and national testing shows that students aren't proficient on the basic skills of the twentieth century and we have yet to begin to assess students' skills and knowledge that are projected as a need in the twenty-first century.

2. How has the purpose of public education changed over time?
   Schools now need to ensure all learners are proficient. This is the first time in history our society has had these elevated expectations written into law.

3. What skills and knowledge will students need to be successful in the twenty-first century?
   Learners will still need the set of basic skills in the core content areas as always. In addition, they will need the twenty-first-century core content of global awareness and financial, civic, health, and technology and information literacy. Accompanying these content skills and knowledge, students should demonstrate the new life skills of working with others, creativity, adaptability, and persistence.

4. What resources and structures will be needed as public education is redesigned for the twenty-first century?
   The educational system needs to ensure a twenty-first-century guaranteed viable curriculum, empower students as partners in their own learning, assess with students to inform instruction, individualize the time/pacing and support of learning, and build capacity in teachers in twenty-first-century skills and knowledge.

• *2* •

Creating the Schools Our Kids Deserve!

Fundamental components in chapter 2:

- Missed Opportunity to Partner with Students
- Blending Essentialism and Progressivism
- Six Levels of System Alignment
- The Proposed Solution
- The Common Moral Purpose
- Preparing the Culture
- The Learner Improvement Cycle
- Key Points in Chapter 2

Guiding Questions for Chapter 2:

1. What opportunities have been missed to improve achievement?
2. What is the philosophical basis for being learner-centered and standards-driven? What are the major components?
3. Why is aligning a school system critical to the success of an initiative?
4. What are the major components of the proposed *Reawakening the learner*?

MISSED OPPORTUNITY TO PARTNER WITH STUDENTS

Public education has missed two partnering opportunities to maximize students' intellectual and personal/social development:

Public education has not invited students to be a partner in their own education; and

Public education has not capitalized on the full potential of being a standards-driven system.

Too often students are passive, compliant workers, not learners, waiting for a teacher to fill their heads or to assign the next packet. Too often standards may appear in the learning objective in the front of the classroom but are not used as an interactive tool to be achieved when a teacher and learner collaborate. *It's the blending of a standards-driven curriculum and learner involvement that will leverage our students to greater achievement.*

Why are the experts thinking of restructuring public education and for what purpose? Does society know what public education needs to look like to serve the needs of all children? Can a twenty-first-century society handle a citizenry who have been educated as partners, and not as products? Can that society adapt itself to the power being unleashed by every learner being proficient? To answer these questions, one must look to the philosophical foundations of public education.

BLENDING ESSENTIALISM AND PROGRESSIVISM

The sense of urgency created in the previous questions have caused a proposed synthesis of two apparently dichotomous philosophies: essentialism and progressivism (Sadker and Sadker 2004). The blending of these two philosophies ensures a new way of looking at learning by mastering priority standards for learners while engaging them as active participants. Our current instructional strategies and curriculum are not working for the current population of learners nor allow the learners to be successful in the twenty-first century. Many districts have tried various programs to raise mastery, but haven't seen measurable change in achievement or increased active learner engagement.

For the twenty-first century, it is necessary to resurrect the blending of progressivism and essentialism into a hybrid philosophy. The concept of *progressive essentialism* was first discussed in an article by Stanley, Smith, and Benne (1943) who described progressive essentialism (remember the time and setting was during World War II) as democratic principles that must be taught through essentialist means to perpetuate society, so that learners can use the skills and knowledge they mastered to ensure the values of a democratic society. By using democratic principles (one person, one vote; majority rules, minority rights), citizens used progressivism to question authority.

Over sixty years later, the authors suggest a reversal of the terms to *essential-progressivism*. By making *progressivism* the noun and *essential* the adjective, the focus is on the individual and the learners are the active participants in mastering the basic and complex skills and knowledge (essential standards) to apply in an ever-changing world. If educational structures can create strong individuals, the result will be a stronger society. States such as Colorado are beginning to restructure their PK–20 system to move away from seat-time requirements and toward a more standards-driven, performance-based system, focused on the whole child (SB 08-212 2008).

In this book, the authors are emphasizing the reform from the current educational focus on essentialism. The current focus in American education is on the essentialist concept of standards and testing, which takes the learners out of the equation. The authors suggest the movement away from the extremes of the spectrum on either end of the continuum to an "inclusive essential-progressivism middle." Due to the current focus on essentialism, the focus of this book is moving from essentialism toward essential-progressivism.

In the continua at the end of Learner Improvement Cycle chapters (chapters 7–10), a progression of skills and knowledge are outlined in order to support the transformation toward essential-progressivism. The *advanced teacher* will be creating the conditions in the classroom for learners to collaboratively show what they know, determine their next learning objectives, and plan for the resources, approach, and materials to accomplish the learning objective.

Learner-Centric Principles

To be learner-centric means that children are engaged in a process where they are partners in learning with their teachers. They accept more responsibility and are actively engaged in the assessing, evaluating, planning, and learning of the standards. Learners are in partnership with the staff in creating a culture that is ready for change, developing a process to create trust so they can doubt incongruent practices, and collectively collaborate to build efficacy.

Without the child's involvement, learning will not be maximized. In 1990, the American Psychological Association (APA) developed learner-centered principles. These were revised in 1997. These fourteen principles are organized and explained in the following chart, under the four factors of: (a) metacognitive and cognitive, (b) motivational and affective, (c) developmental and social, and (d) individual differences (APA 1997).

Table 2.1. Summary of APA's Learner-Centered Principles (1997)

Factors to Develop in Learners	APA Principles	Summary of Each APA Principle A successful learner:
Cognitive and Metacognitive Factors	Nature of the learning process	Constructs meaning from information and experience as an intentional process.
	Goals of the learning process	Is goal-directed over time and with support.
	Construction of knowledge	Links new and existing knowledge meaningfully.
	Strategic thinking	Uses a repertoire of thinking and reasoning strategies.
	Thinking about thinking	Reflects on how he thinks and learns.
	Context of learning	Understands how she is influenced by culture, technology, and instructional practices.
Motivational and Affective Factors	Motivational and emotional influences on learning	Is motivated to learn by his emotional states, beliefs, interests, goals, and habits of thinking.
	Intrinsic motivation to learn	Is intrinsically motivated by novelty, difficulty, relevancy, personal choice, and control.
	Effects of motivation on effort	Is motivated to learn and exert effort without coercion.
Developmental and Social Factors	Developmental influences on learning	Learns in an environment where physical, intellectual, emotional, and social domains are taken into account.
	Social influences on learning	Learns best when positive social interactions, interpersonal relations, and communication with others are in place.
Individual Differences Factors	Individual differences in learning	Is aware of learning-styles preferences and is able to expand or modify them if necessary.
	Learning and diversity	Learns in an environment where differences of linguistic, cultural, and social backgrounds are taken into account.
	Standards and assessment	Responds to high and challenging standards and is appropriately assessed on those standards.

Standards-Driven Learning Environments

Creating a standards-driven learning environment means that students understand exactly what they need to know and be able to do. This is done within a
system where learners, at their own pace, make progress based on the mastery of
a guaranteed, viable curriculum.

In Colorado, this process has been a fifteen-year journey to realize its potential in new legislation, Colorado Achievement Plan for Kids (CAP4K, SB
08-212). In 1997, when the standards movement was first being defined through
a Goals 2000 grant, the Standards Based Education (SBE) Design Team, from
the Centennial Board of Cooperative Educational Services (Centennial BOCES),
illustrated this quest through the metaphor of climbing a mountain:

> They labeled the initial ascent of the mountain as being an *Emerging SBE
> System* (standards-referenced). An Emerging SBE System is one where
> the "curriculum alignment to standards is in progress, assessment of stu-
> dent performance on standards occurs, and students and parents have an
> awareness of standards" (Centennial BOCES 1997).
>
> The middle of the trek up the mountain is a *Transitional SBE System*
> (standards-based), which is described when "instructional planning and
> curriculum decision-making are driven by alignment with standards and
> benchmarks; assessment is aligned with standards and benchmarks; and
> teachers and learners see a clear correlation between instructional activi-
> ties, assessments, and the standards and benchmarks."
>
> The summit of the mountain is becoming the *Comprehensive SBE System*
> (standards-driven) (Centennial BOCES 1997), which means "instruc-
> tional planning, decision-making, curriculum, and learning activities for
> groups and for individual students is driven by data analysis of student
> performance on standards and benchmarks; assessment informs instruc-
> tion; all stakeholders share common goals of individual student achieve-
> ment of standards and work together to that end."

For the purposes of this book, a "standards-driven system" is one where learners drive the pace of their learning, monitor their progress, and contribute to
the relevance of the mastery of the curriculum based on the district's defined
essential learnings.

Building Leadership Capacity for a Learner-Centric, Standards-Driven System

In discussing building leadership capacity, Linda Lambert (1998, 12) defines
leadership as the involvement of many stakeholder groups in "broad-based, skillful participation in the work of leadership." The principalship continua in this

book help to define skillful participation. The continua are a tool for individuals to assess their own skill set, with the goal of being engaged in collaborative inquiry, reflective practice, and innovation to raise achievement (Lambert 1998).

To begin this process, principals and staff need to assess where their school is currently functioning on the continua. Looking through the lens of ensuring a common moral purpose, being ready to change, having trust-to-doubt current practices, and a having a culture of collective efficacy enables the leadership of a school to place themselves on the continua and set SMART goals to move the school to the next developmental stage. These PDCA plans are then put into action, monitored, and adjusted based on key performance indicators.

To establish the conditions and culture in a school that will ensure *proficiency for all*, the continua center around the theme of involving students in their learning. To build this capacity, plans must be created to foster a skill set during professional development. This professional development is based on creating new knowledge and skills in the system (principals-teachers-learners), utilizing an essential-progressivist approach that is embedded in the Learner Improvement Cycle. This skill-building model must be extended to the learners so they begin to "live" the twenty-first-century skills they need to thrive.

This can't be done in the isolation of the classroom or the school. Too many schools have tried and failed because they hit barriers when interacting with other entities within the system. There must be alignment within the entire educational system.

SIX LEVELS OF SYSTEM ALIGNMENT

Michael Fullan (2005) discusses tri-level alignment between the state, district, and school in order to create system sustainability. Digging deeper into each of those levels and subdividing the three can clearly define the roles. It can be argued that there are six levels of alignment that support the learner in the classroom.

Beginning with the learner and creating alignment in the system, districts must then align policy and practices from the learner through the personnel in the classroom, the school, the central office, the District Board of Education, the state legislators, and Department of Education. Learners, as a group, may be implied in Fullan's model, but need to be discussed more overtly. Parents and community members are included in the process through contributing to the shared vision of the district and school and through participating in the democratic process of electing the District Board of Education and state legislators. They also attend accountability meetings and board meetings to give input during the process.

The alignment of systems at the school, classroom, and learner level need to be put into a greater context of state and district systems. In an ideal world, for the learners' sake, these six systems would be aligned:

1. *The learner.* To begin with the end in mind, one must appreciate that the learners themselves are a system. All other systems must align to the needs of the learner. To maximize their education, the learners must partner with the adults. One way this manifests itself is by ensuring that the vision of the system aligns with the needs of the individuals. Learners must work together with each other and with adults to assess their current level of knowledge and skills, be an active participant in the evaluating and planning of their education, and be accountable for one another in a learning community to assure all reach proficiency. In order for learners to be postsecondary and workplace ready, they must demonstrate proficiency in the expected skills and knowledge.

2. *The classroom.* At the classroom level, teachers and learners must reach consensus about their common moral purpose to make their shared vision become a reality. This translates into teachers needing to help learners define and monitor their progress on the agreed-upon standards. Teachers must collaborate *with* learners to delineate what students need to know and be able to do, so the children can learn and monitor their goals independently.

   Teachers need to *create the conditions* for learners to assess what they must learn, evaluate their assessment results, set and monitor goals based on the data, and engage in activities that will further the students' learning. Teachers must also engage learners in being able to define and monitor the creation of individual and classroom codes of conduct and use tools to give feedback. This adds to Robert Marzano's work (2007) by including learner ownership to the three components of an effective teacher: using strategies in (a) effective instruction, (b) classroom management, and (c) classroom curriculum design.

3. *The school.* The most "bang for the buck" in achievement is when a student has an effective school and teacher (Marzano 2003). A student achieving at the 50th percentile is able to reach achievement at the 96th percentile in two years with both an effective school and teacher. According to Marzano (2003), the meta-analysis of research factors into five categories of an effective school: (a) sustaining a guaranteed, viable curriculum; (b) setting challenging goals and providing effective feedback; (c) soliciting parental and community involvement; (d) creating a safe and orderly environment; and (e) demanding collegiality and professionalism.

In a loose-tight system (DuFour et al. 2004), the district's shared vision becomes the goal (tight) that all schools must accomplish, and the leadership of each school has the flexibility (loose) to consider the characteristics of their school and current research to create a plan of action. Schools and classrooms must align to the district's shared vision based on learners' needs. Principals and teachers must align with the district's learner-centered shared vision in order to activate that vision with learners through the use of research-based practices.

4. *The central office.* In some districts, the *superintendent* is the only person who is held responsible for the workings of the district. The *superintendency* comprises the members of the extended cabinet in the central office, who collect information, provide input, and deliberate on decisions made for the district (personal communication with Roberta Selleck, September 23, 2008).

   What district central office staff must do is take the district shared vision and put goals and action plans in place to make it become a reality. They provide service so that each learner has an effective school with an effective teacher. The central office staff, with the help of school personnel, must align systems and resources within and between Learning Services, Human Resources, Business and Finance, and Auxiliary Services toward these ends.

   Systems within the district must be created to monitor progress and, if practices are out of alignment, adjust to realign the processes with the goals. Processes and policies must be defined and reviewed so they are "systemic" throughout the PK–12 system, and consistent no matter who delivers them. This involves the creation of quality flowcharts, toolkits, and common practices on which all staff are trained and progress is monitored. Practices that no longer fit into the system must be eliminated.

5. *The district Board of Education.* School Boards of Education and superintendents must create a public engagement process to bring a representative group of stakeholders together to define the *shared vision* for the district and provide the necessary resources to ensure its fruition. A *shared vision* is a statement that guides the activities of the district and is shared by its stakeholders. For example, in Colorado, HB 07-1118 has recently outlined an engagement process in which each community needs to define the criteria for a high-school graduate. Through shared vision and strategic planning, this can become the blueprint for systemic change, alignment, and improvement.

   The state defines the process; the district determines the content in a locally controlled state such as Colorado. It is imperative that a governance board sets a shared vision, creates policy, plans for resource allocation, and monitors results. As a member of the community, with access to local, state, and national trends, members of the board can bring potential solutions to district issues.

If a Board of Education observes a policy governance model, members can bring these ideas forward and can become a lever for change. Boards must work through their only employee, the superintendent of the district, and work together as a unit to collectively make decisions that are in the best interest of the learners in the district, avoiding their individual agendas.

6. *The state legislators and Department of Education.* In order to ensure system support, backward-planning must be utilized to align the practices from the learner to the state. State statute and policy is written to require accountability and compliance and respond to the needs of constituents. Statutes require actions from districts, based on the district's interpretation of appropriate implementation for their district. It is important to note our political process allows for us to influence state statute and policy to ensure alignment with the district's learner-centered shared vision.

Examples in Colorado and Arizona highlight the shift in thinking at the state level. Due to the current postgraduation results in Colorado (poor graduation rates, increased remediation at the college level, and feedback from employers), legislation was written to support change. Current legislation (CAP4K, SB 08-212) in the state of Colorado shifts the focus of the relationship between the Colorado Department of Education and school districts from accountability and compliance to support in order to assure learners have met standards. Furthermore, SB 08-212 has defined a process to reinvigorate standards-based education and truly create a performance-based system, instead of one based on seat-time. The legislation focuses on the whole child and being learner-centric as a strategy to attain standards from school readiness to mastery for postsecondary and workplace readiness.

In Arizona, the Arizona Community Foundation (2008) created a report, *Educating Arizona*, recommending that the state move from a system that bases promotion on age and time to one that is based on performance, with metrics designed to measure progress while holding everyone accountable.

So, with six-level alignment, the authors come back to the essential question of this book: how does our society create schools to ensure *proficiency for all* learners to meet the ever-changing needs in the twenty-first century?

THE PROPOSED SOLUTION

The authors propose involving learners in schooling. A change in philosophy (learner-centered moral purpose), leads to a changed culture (readiness, trust-to-doubt, and collective efficacy), which leads to learner-centric practice in the classroom (Learner Improvement Cycle), which leads to increased results (mastery of twenty-first-century skills and *proficiency for all* learners).

In chapter 1, the case was made to change the current system. It was discussed that NCLB (2001) requires all students to be proficient; therefore, it will require a new system with a new purpose. This will not be a tweaking of the old, but a second-order change of a very traditional, time-honored system. A second-order change is one which "breaks with the past, conflicts with prevailing norms and values, requires the acquisition of new knowledge and skills, and requires resources currently not available to those responsible for the innovation" (Marzano, Waters, and McNulty 2005, 113), and may be resisted by those who don't share the perspective of the needed change.

The new set of twenty-first-century skills (Partnership for the 21st Century 2008) requires learners to be flexible, take initiative, and be accountable. Our old factory-based educational model is not set up to allow learners this adaptability. Even though people report dissatisfaction with our current educational system, efforts made to overhaul the system have been faced with resistance.

The agrarian, industrial educational system does not have the philosophical underpinnings, and thus the structure, to adapt to these new expectations. Never in our educational history were all children expected to reach proficiency while anticipating public education to prepare learners for a very ambiguous future. Predicting the occupational needs of our nation in ten years and creating a school system for learners to be prepared for that future is a major challenge.

In chapter 2, as a part of the proposed solution, it is suggested that moving away from philosophical camps of essentialism and progressivism to the synthesis of these two philosophies is critical. To create a system to have all learners achieve proficiency, educators must know what society wants them to know and be able to do (essentialism) and give the learners ownership of the achievement of those goals (progressivism). Becoming learner-centric AND standards-driven will support learners achieving a set of twenty-first-century skills while becoming partners in their educational process and begin creating solutions to the ambiguity of an uncertain future.

THE COMMON MORAL PURPOSE

In section 2 (chapter 3), the authors insist that our educational system must have a common moral purpose to deal with the changing demographics and slow-

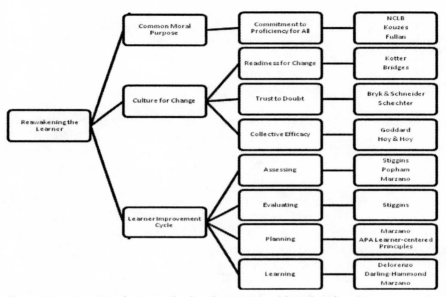

Figure 2.1. Tree Map for Reawakening the Learner with Major Theorists

growing local, state, and national test scores. School staffs must identify their individual moral purpose and then reach consensus on a common moral purpose for their organization. Fullan (2005) says moral purpose should raise the expectations of achievement, of staff performance, and the culture of the organization. The continua in chapter 3 outline a process for staff to PDCA the development of their individual and common moral purpose.

PREPARING THE CULTURE

In section 3 (chapters 4 through 6), the conditions necessary to make this kind of monumental change are discussed. It involves preparing the culture of the organization for change. The staff must prepare itself for the change process. To do this it must have a trusting culture so it can doubt practices that no longer fit in the organization. It must also build collective efficacy in order to accomplish difficult goals.

Readiness for Change

To be ready for change, the people within an organization must understand the urgency for change and begin to build a guiding coalition to carry out the change (Kotter 1996). Readiness for change is tackled in chapter 4. Supporting the staff's transitions during this change process and preparing the organization for the outcomes of a first- or second-order change (Marzano, Waters, and McNulty 2005) is the keystone in this course of action.

Trust-to-Doubt Process

Chapter 5 discusses how the progression to create a trusting culture in a school is vital to the conversations that will follow once the change process begins. When relational trust is present: (a) it creates a moral imperative to take on the hard work and spread it across the organization; (b) it reduces the risk and makes it safe to experiment with new practices; and (c) it leads to academic productivity (Bryk and Schneider 2002). Our concept of *trust-to-doubt* is predicated on the establishment of a culture of trust that allows the participants to doubt, or call into question, current practices that are ineffective or misaligned to the common moral purpose. This ability to doubt must be available at every level of the organization. This reframes *doubt* from its current negative connotation to a tool for productive, collaborative inquiry. The motives for doubt must be based in a belief that by doubting the system, it will improve our practices.

Collective Efficacy

Staff members must have the belief system that they can achieve greatness together. This belief system is built through the confidence they have the skills and knowledge and (a) are empowered to accomplish what is being asked of them, (b) having other successful experiences that they can draw upon, and (c) seeing the change in action in a similar situation (Hoy, Smith, and Sweetland 2002). The continua that address creating a culture of learner-centric collective efficacy are detailed in chapter 6.

THE LEARNER IMPROVEMENT CYCLE

In section 4, the components of the Learner Improvement Cycle will be addressed in chapters 7 through 10, which propose changes in practice at the classroom and school level. The Learner Improvement Cycle arose out of the work of Richard C. Owen's teaching-learning cycle (1999) and the continuous improvement cycle from the American Society for Quality (2004). Owen's Teaching and Learning Cycle consists of the elements of (a) assessing, (b) evaluating, (c) planning, and (d) teaching and learning. The authors have created an adaptation to adjust the components to a Learner Improvement Cycle. Each component has an embedded continuous improvement cycle (plan, do, check, adjust) to refine each practice which focuses more on the learner and the learning.

Section 5 (chapter 11) calls for a national dialogue to create a transformation in public education that ensures the creation of an educational system where all students become active learners and are given the time and resources to be proficient. It has to be more than lengthening the school day and school year in the current system (Duncan [2009], as cited in Meyer [2009]).

In transition to section 2 (chapter 3), the reader will begin the journey of creating the schools our learners deserve! Chapter 3 explains the detail of how to identify individual moral purpose and reach consensus on a common moral purpose. The journey begins by creating a common moral purpose.

Key Points in Chapter 2:

1. What opportunities have been missed to improve achievement?
   In teacher-only directed classrooms, students become the product of the teacher's instruction, instead of a partner in their own learning. Students need to understand what they need to learn, know their progress on that learning, and use their interests and motivation to achieve proficiency.
2. What is the philosophical basis for being learner-centered and standards-driven? What are the major components?
   Two dominant philosophical tenets, essentialism and progressivism, once seen as dichotomous, must be blended for students to have input into their mastery of a set of standards prescribed by the state or local authority. The American Psychological Association has prescribed a set of learner-centered principles as guidelines for this accomplishment.
3. Why is aligning a system critical to the success of an initiative?
   The system can be a barrier to any change initiative. The system must be in philosophical alignment from the student through the state department. This ensures a systemic and consistent implementation.
4. What are the major components of *Reawakening the Learner*?
   The changes to a school culture are organized through creating a common moral purpose, a readiness for change, trust-to-doubt, and collective efficacy. The substantive change comes through adapting the teaching-learning cycle into the Learner Improvement Cycle that requires a major role for the student. The individual's response in the change process must be supported. Continuous improvement is furthered through a PDCA process.

Section 2

THE COMMON MORAL PURPOSE

Make your work to be in keeping with your [common moral] purpose.

—Leonardo da Vinci

In the following chapter, the authors describe the developmental process of the first requisite step in any change process, moving through the continuum from an individual moral purpose to a common moral purpose.

The beginning stakeholder or school represents those who don't operate under an individual moral purpose and have not yet begun work on the common moral purpose.

Moving along the continuum is the *developing stakeholder or school*, which cultivates the individual and common moral purposes, respectively. *The developing stakeholder* communicates the moral purpose to others.

Proficient stakeholder or school has tightly aligned individual and common moral purposes. The *proficient stakeholder* indicates when other's beliefs or actions are in conflict with the common moral purpose.

The *advanced stakeholder or school* develops a common moral purpose and aligns practice. The *advanced stakeholder* influences others if the moral purpose is violated.

• 3 •

Developing Moral Purpose

Fundamental components of chapter 3:

- Twenty-First-Century Moral Purpose
- Role of Learners in Moral Purpose
- Individual and Common Beliefs and Behaviors
- Continuous Improvement of Moral Purpose
- Individual Stakeholder Moral Purpose Continua
- Common Moral Purpose Continua
- Moral Purpose/Shared Vision: Conversations with Stakeholders
- Key Points in Chapter 3

Guiding Questions in Chapter 3:

1. What do you think should be the twenty-first-century common moral purpose for education?
2. What's the learner's role in actualizing the moral purpose of her education?
3. How does a system help stakeholders identify their individual moral purpose in order to reach consensus on a common moral purpose? How can a system reinforce the alignment of behaviors with beliefs?

TWENTY-FIRST-CENTURY MORAL PURPOSE

Public education's moral purpose is to provide an educational environment that creates *proficiency for all* to prepare learners to be productive citizens in the twenty-first century. The bell-shaped curve is no longer a desirable distribution of student achievement where there are acceptable losses and children are permitted to advance in the curriculum without mastering the material.

In the early 1990s, the concept of the "J" curve (Spady 1994) suggested a new format for learning in which mastery of curriculum was expected for all, given enough time and support. This thinking is compatible with Michael Fullan's (2005, 15) concept of moral purpose which should "(1) raise the bar and close the gap; (2) treat people with demanding respect; and (3) alter the social environment for the better."

Raising Expectations for All

It is believed that *all* deserve an education and should be given the time and resources that prepare them for their future. No individual should be less than proficient due to their ethnicity, language, disability, gender, or socioeconomic status. Data must continually be disaggregated to create urgency and monitor the progress of action plans, in order to move the bar toward *proficiency for all* and thus narrow the gap between subgroups. Traditionally, the achievement gap is defined as the difference between the achievement of identified ethnic or gender groups. The "new achievement gap" is the gap between where an individual *is* performing and the desired performance standard of proficiency and above.

Insistent Leadership

Leaders must be the keepers of the common moral purpose and confront staff and the system when learners aren't held to these high standards. Creating tools, processes, and systems to hold all stakeholders accountable for all results are imperative. This can be accomplished by creating PDCA templates that filter all proposals through the lens of the common moral purpose. Educators are often asked to implement a well-intentioned program that does not further the accomplishment of the shared vision.

Now in the age of accountability, all of these requests cannot be granted and still focus on the *main thing* (Covey, Merrill, and Merrill 1994) that aligns to our common moral purpose. Insistent leadership in the school, whether it's the principal or teacher-leaders, must supply the pressure and support to align policies and procedures to the common moral purpose and provide resources (financial, time, human) to accomplish this end.

Creating Citizens Who Are Interdependent

The authors agree with Michael Fullan when he says that public education needs to alter the social environment for the better. Upon further discussion with Fullan, he says society needs to develop citizens who feel accountable for one another's learning (personal e-mail, July 11, 2008). This is accomplished through collaboration between and among learners, teachers, administrators, and the public. This collaboration creates a feeling of responsibility and interdependence while contributing to the success of our society.

Learners, who know and can do more than the previous generation, can contribute to others in the school (microcosm). They then contribute to the world (macrocosm), and make the world a better place than they found it. Having older learners mentor younger learners, whether it's about the school's moral purpose or academics, will provide a mastery experience (Woolfolk 2008). This shows learners that if they can succeed in one aspect of their lives (school), they can take that mastery experience and apply it to new challenging experiences in their lives and succeed.

ROLE OF LEARNERS IN MORAL PURPOSE

Recall that a new paradigm, essential-progressivism, was discussed in detail in the second chapter. The blending of essentialism and progressivism engages the learner in a prescribed set of standards and puts a premium on applying the standards learned in school to authentic situations. An essential-progressivist's moral purpose requires partnering with learners in order for them to master a set of essential learnings in an engaging classroom environment.

Learners need to be a part of the process of reflecting about their own moral purpose and engaged in creating the common moral purpose in the school. The new moral purpose of public education is partnering with learners, with sufficient *time* and *support*, so *all learners are proficient* in twenty-first-century skills and knowledge. Once learners have defined a moral purpose and feel a part of the common moral purpose, they are motivated to be partners in their own learning.

INDIVIDUAL AND COMMON BELIEFS AND BEHAVIORS

In examining the continua of moral purpose, shown in Table 3.1, the reader will notice the disconnection between individual beliefs and behaviors. Administrators lead schools where there is a conflict of behaviors exhibited among staff members, but no conversations ever occur to uncover the root causes of the conflict. It is the staff's belief system that causes the tension to exist from the philosophical conflict between essentialism and progressivism.

Staff members, who have philosophical differences, play out their own belief systems in their school behaviors. For existing staff members, it is important to help them understand their own values and moral purpose for being in public education. For recruiting new staff, it is important to probe candidates for self-awareness, a realization of an individual moral purpose and alignment to the organization's common moral purpose. There needs to become a transparency of how their individual moral purpose manifests itself in behaviors.

In Jim Kouzes' research (2008) on how much do employees' values equate to organizational commitment, he states that the best-case scenario is to have clarity about your own values and those of the organizations (6.26 on a 7-point Likert scale). Next in priority, he found that commitment to the organization is greater when employees have clarity about their own personal values before having clarity about the organization's values (6.12). After that, having no clarity in their personal values but clarity in organization's values (4.87) and having no clarity in personal values or organizational values (4.90) equates to an equal amount of commitment to the organization.

As a result of this thinking, it is important for the principalship to assist staff members in identifying their own value system prior to reaching consensus for the organization's values. This will lead to more commitment to the organization.

In many schools, there are few conversations with the staff to create a shared vision or moral purpose to work out the differences in a staff's belief system. Often the conversations that are held sound more like conflicts in discipline philosophies, instructional strategies, and even grading systems.

In a healthy system, a common moral purpose is developed through a process that involves all stakeholders. The components of the common moral purpose are backward-planned into an action plan. So when a staff comes together, its members understand their foundational basis for all decisions and must align organizational practices to this purpose. If the moral purpose is only a belief and not accompanied by behaviors, then it's just a slogan. When the moral purpose is believed by all staff members and aligned with practices, then staff will enlist and invest in the common moral purpose.

The staff must have a process in place that will occur when its members feel the moral purpose of the organization is ignored or violated. A robust trust-to-doubt process can uncover the misalignment between beliefs and behaviors in a safe and trusting environment. Communication and conflict-resolution skills may have to be developed prior to issues arising. This will be discussed further in chapter 5.

CONTINUOUS IMPROVEMENT OF MORAL PURPOSE

The following continua have been produced to guide the thinking of teachers and the principalship in creating a common moral purpose. The principalship must create a PDCA with a focus on creating a common moral purpose for the entire school community.

1. The *planning* phase involves looking at barriers and opportunities and having staff, learners, and community members share their individual moral purposes. This involves looking for themes among the individual moral purposes of the staff and creating a plan to reach resolution on the differences. Then a plan can be created to design a common moral purpose for the staff and identify KPIs to monitor and measure implementation.
2. The *doing* phase involves using tools and processes to determine common ideals and writing a set of "We Believe" statements for the school. This process must involve learners. The staff, community, and learners then define what the common moral purpose looks like in practice. The set of "We Believe" statements then becomes the guidelines by which all decisions are made.

   Staff members who don't align their behaviors with this common moral purpose will continue to be influenced by the group or may have to seek other environments that better align with their individual moral purpose. A proficient school then hires staff for these beliefs and behaviors. The older learners influence new learners as they join the school.
3. Then staff members must *check* their current practices and policies against their common belief system and KPIs in cycle times.
4. The staff and learners *adjust* any practices that don't align and shorten cycle times to increase effectiveness.

Table 3.1. Individual Stakeholder Moral Purpose Continua

	Category	Beginning Stakeholder	Developing Stakeholder	Proficient Stakeholder	Advanced Stakeholder Meets All Proficient Criteria, Plus
PLAN	Planning for identifying own moral purpose	• Hasn't created a plan to identify his own moral purpose nor identify behaviors he exhibits that would align with his moral purpose.	• Determines root causes of defining a moral purpose. • Looks for leverage points to improve results. • Begins to talk about a plan and having a moral purpose but hasn't created a plan to identify own moral purpose.	• Creates a plan to identify own moral purpose. • Identifies KPIs for individual moral purpose.	• Shares plans and processes with colleagues and pushes on the principalship to align to a common moral purpose.
DO	Identifying beliefs	• Can't explain that having a moral purpose is important; or hasn't developed own moral purpose.	• Begins to develop own moral purpose that aligns with new purpose of public education.	• Reads and discusses educational philosophy, how do children learn, reason for becoming a teacher • Develops own moral purpose (I Believe) that aligns with new purpose of public education.	• Has a strong moral purpose that *all* learners can be proficient that guides all decisions. • Treats people with demanding respect (supportive, responsive, and demanding) to accomplish new moral purpose of public education.

CHECK	Assessing alignment of behaviors to beliefs	• Behaves in a manner inconsistent with new moral purpose of public education.	• Begins to see that some actions don't align with own moral purpose and of public education.	• Self-assesses for alignment of beliefs and behaviors through a 360-degree process.	• Influences others if own moral purpose is violated.
ADJUST	Aligning behaviors to beliefs	• Accepts "the disconnect" between own moral beliefs and own behaviors.	• Experiences cognitive dissonance when behaviors conflict with own moral purpose.	• Brings beliefs and behaviors into congruence. • Behaves in a manner that is mostly consistent with own moral purpose and of public education.	• Behaves in a manner that is consistent with own moral purpose and of public education. • Tells stakeholders why they do what they do.

Table 3.2. Common Moral Purpose Continua

	Category	Beginning School	Developing School	Proficient School	Advanced Stakeholder Meets All Proficient Criteria, Plus
PLAN	Planning to create a common moral purpose	• Hasn't created a plan to identify common moral purpose nor identified needed behaviors to align with common moral purpose.	• Determines root causes of current status of common moral purpose. • Looks for leverage points to improve results. • Begins to talk about a plan and having a common moral purpose but hasn't created a plan.	• Creates a plan and process to reach consensus to identify common moral purpose • Develops Key Performance Indicators (KPIs) that evidence implementation and success.	• Shares plans and processes and pushes on system to align to a common moral purpose.
DO	Creating a common moral purpose	• Doesn't address staff members when his/her individual moral purpose doesn't agree with common moral purpose	• Develops or identifies individual moral purpose. • Begins to influence staff members who do not believe in common moral purpose.	• Uses personal moral purpose • Reads and discusses educational philosophy, how do children learn, reason for public education • Reaches consensus on "We Believe" statements as common moral purpose. • Defines what common moral purpose looks like in practice.	• Merges many strong individual moral purposes into a strong common moral purpose. • Enhances common moral purpose through alignment of processes and programs. • Continues to view proposals through lens of common moral purpose.

DO	Developing congruence between common moral purpose and behaviors	• Hasn't aligned a common moral purpose to behaviors.	• Begins to have conversations about common moral purpose and behaviors.	• Articulates and uses their common moral purpose to guide decision-making. • Influences those who do not align with common moral purpose.	• Articulates both <u>what</u> they do and <u>why</u> they do it.
	Ensuring learner involvement in common moral purpose	• Doesn't involve learners in creation and continuation of school's common moral purpose.	• Shares moral purpose with learners. No learner involvement in creation.	• Creates common moral purpose with stakeholders and learners.	• Alters social environment for better. • Involves older learners in sustaining school's moral purpose by modeling and teaching younger learners.
CHECK	Gathering and assessing common moral purpose progress	• Doesn't identify or check KPIs in any cycles.	• Gathers anecdotal information on progress made on common moral purpose.	• Gathers and analyzes measureable data aligned to KPIs in periodic cycle times. • Assesses for alignment of common moral purpose and behaviors.	• Gathers and analyzes measureable data aligned to KPIs in shortened cycle times.

(continued)

Table 3.2. *(continued)*

	Category	Beginning School	Developing School	Proficient School	Advanced Stakeholder Meets All Proficient Criteria, Plus
ADJUST	Making adjustments	• Doesn't adjust alignment to common moral purpose based on feedback.	• Adjust only on anecdotal data.	• Brings common moral purpose and behaviors into congruence with KPIs. • Reinforces common moral purpose.	• Makes adjustments on a quicker basis based on shortened cycle times based on KPIs.

Suggested evidences:

➤ Agendas/posters/ pictures/ research used of learner, parent, and staff involvement in the creation of the common moral purpose

➤ Increased numbers of learners being proficient (*proficiency for all*).

➤ Staff and learners have personal moral purposes that they share with others–"I believe" statements

➤ Stated process for learners to sustain the vision and mission with new and younger learners

➤ Self-evaluation, with multiple cycle times, on the continua has moved toward advanced status.

➤ PDCA plans for the implementation of creating individual and common moral purposes with KPI's and cycle times.

➤ "We Believe" statements that unpack the common moral purpose, signed by all staff and learners make the common moral purpose actionable and renewed annually.

➤ Template to filter decisions and behaviors through the common moral purpose- Series of questions.

➤ Continuous improvement process that evaluates the progress made on common moral purpose: Plus/delta.

➤ Symbolic reinforcement of the moral purpose- agendas, celebrations.

➤ Staff and learners can state the common moral purpose and cite examples of it in practice.

MORAL PURPOSE/SHARED VISION:
CONVERSATIONS WITH THE STAKEHOLDERS

(In District 50, the staff and learners created "shared visions," not "common moral purposes." The authors used the term that stakeholders are familiar with in their questioning, but the terms are interchangeable.)

Voices of the Principals

Question: "How did you move your school from individual belief systems to one shared belief system?" The summary of interviews with four principals who were implementing a shared vision and inspiring a moral purpose all expressed that it truly must be shared by all stakeholder groups.

Previously, Kelly Williams, principal at Scott Carpenter Middle School, said, "I came up with the vision and shared it." Now she has turned the process over to teachers, who coordinated the efforts to gather input from colleagues, parents, and students. They gathered this information through affinity diagrams at registration and back-to-school nights. This resulted in a truly shared document that when in times of trouble she was advised by Rich Delorenzo from the ReInventing Schools Coalition (RISC) to go back and recommit to it. "It is truly a sacred document now."

Chris Benisch, the principal at Harris Park Elementary, sees the power in the systems alignment of a shared vision from the district level to the classroom. He believes an asset to this process is that the district-shift is so systemic that staff members have realized that they can't always do what they've always done. "We're doing this all together because the ship's leaving and if you're not on board, you'll be left."

In order to accomplish a shared vision, assistant principal Sarah Gould at Hodgkins Elementary described the shared visioning process they led their staff through to differentiate between polite conversation, true dialogue, and letting go of assumptions. This allowed them to "check their egos at the door" and create a vision for the school where the students' needs came first.

As Benisch concluded, ultimately the purpose for creating a shared vision is: "We have to do this for the kids."

Voices of the Teachers

Question: "How has reaching consensus on the moral purpose/shared vision for your school changed the practice in your school?" Teachers responded that a school staff needs to follow a specific process where everyone gets to share their opinion. These opinions are then categorized and power voted to determine priorities. Jennifer Rizzo, a Scott Carpenter Middle School teacher, described that they then took those priorities to back-to-school night to their parents. "We realize the importance of consistency in our school; if students are moving between classes, we need to be consistent."

A shared vision, whether it happens at the school level or the classroom level, needs to be created by the group who has to implement it. All teachers agree that the school vision needs to have input from the teachers. As Robin Kietzmann, a teacher at Harris Park Elementary, put it, it's "different for our principals, they have to let the staff come up with the shared vision." When creating a classroom shared vision it must come from the kids.

Greg Russo, a teacher at Shaw Heights Middle School, described the process that he and his teammate, Anne Marie Dadley, used on their team to create a classroom shared vision. As a team, they used the "5 Whys" to discuss the purpose, got the students' input and reached consensus using a consens-o-gram. Kids felt like they had input and when teachers call the students on not living up to the shared vision, they were a lot more responsive since they had input on it.

Rizzo concluded that a shared vision builds community: "Shared vision is a way to put an umbrella over the whole school."

Voices of the Learners

Question: "How were you involved in creating the shared vision for your class?" Learners' responses varied from none to a very specific process. Anna (a pseudonym), a middle-school student, described the process she went through as a representative of her advisory class. She said reps were chosen from each advisory class and went to the library. They were taught about what a shared vision was and came back to their class and taught the class how to do a shared vision. As a result of having a school and classroom shared vision, students have recognized a change in school practices and teacher behavior.

Students reported learning from their teacher, who seemed to care more this year, when they needed it. They also reported more peer teaching and learning, which they weren't allowed to do much of in the past. Penny (a pseudonym), an elementary student, said when what she liked most about this year was working with her peers; "I would try to motivate them and tutor them."

Learners reported being proud of themselves as learners, and being more confident. Anna reported that she loved the "new system where they get to work at our own pace, get help from those who know it, reach higher levels, keep going and going, where we almost know everything."

Voices of the Parents

Question: What differences are you seeing in your child based on the shared vision of this school and class? Parents reported all their children being more confident and responsible. Jason Reynolds, a parent at Scott Carpenter Middle School, said his daughter had "accountability for herself, she ran student-led conferences. The kids drive themselves. I don't have to go to the school for a problem with a student or a teacher; my daughter takes care of it herself. Her motivation has increased."

Tomasita Perri agreed. She was amazed at conferences and commented that "they should have had this when we were in school." Reynolds added they like to work in groups, do homework in groups more often, and use each other's strengths. This is "important in today's world as most businesses work in teams."

Key Points in Chapter 3:

1. What do you think should be the twenty-first-century common moral purpose for education?
   The authors believe that NCLB has the correct moral purpose (although may not have the correct action plan) of proficiency for all but lacks the focus on twenty-first-century skills and knowledge.

2. What's the learner's role in actualizing the moral purpose of their education?
   Up until this time, students were expected to be passive and compliant in their learning at school. This needs to change. Students need to be actively engaged in their own education in order to be learners inside and outside of structured schooling. They need to learn the tools and processes of how to be learners anytime they have a question or a problem.

3. How does a system help stakeholders identify their individual moral purpose in order to reach consensus on a common moral purpose? How can a system reinforce the alignment of behaviors with beliefs?
   The system needs to create a PDCA to identify individual stakeholder's moral purpose and then synthesize all those individual beliefs into a common moral purpose that is in the best interests of students. This common moral purpose should be built by consensus and stakeholders should hold each other accountable for its realization.

Section 3

THE CULTURE OF
CONTINUOUS IMPROVEMENT

Without change, something sleeps inside us, and seldom awakens. The sleeper must awaken.

—Frank Herbert

The following three chapters describe the components of a school culture necessary to prepare for change, embed change in an aligned practice, and sustain continuous improvement.

Beginning schools do not have the recognition, capacity, or skills to prepare themselves for change.

The *developing school* knows it needs to change and is building capacity in itself to adjust its practices.

A *proficient school* has the skills and knowledge to be ready for change, questions the status quo, and has built collective efficacy.

The *advanced schools* gather data to seek out problems rather than wait for them to occur. They have built systems for sustainability and continuous improvement. Learners are involved in the improvement processes of the school.

• *4* •

Readiness for Change

Fundamental Components of Chapter 4:

- Current Practices that Show Need for Readiness for Change
- Collaborative PDCA on Readiness for Change
- Creating the Culture of Readiness for Change Continua
- Readiness for Change: Conversations with Stakeholders
- Key Points in Chapter 4

Guiding Questions in Chapter 4:

1. How do you plan for a change culture?
2. How does creating a culture of change prepare the adults for the twenty-first-century skills the students will need to learn?

CREATING THE CULTURE FOR READINESS FOR CHANGE

Michael Fullan (2001) believes, and the authors concur, that leaders must understand the need for change along with creating a common moral purpose or else they will slip into moral martyrdom. This means that change has to be more than a vision; the principalship must have the skill set to make the vision become a reality. This involves understanding the change process and preparing staff to be ready for change; in this case, preparing the school culture so all learners will be proficient. School cultures have been reticent to change and therefore teachers do not have many of the twenty-first-century skills of adaptability, flexibility, and persistence throughout the PDCA cycle for change.

For the purposes of this chapter, the readiness for change is preparing stakeholders to move from a teacher-directed classroom to the learner-centric classroom (the Learner Improvement Cycle). For most this will be a second-order change. A second-order change means a "dramatic departure from the expected, both in defining the given problem and in finding the solution" (Marzano, Waters, and McNulty 2005, 66).

CURRENT PRACTICES THAT SHOW
NEED FOR READINESS FOR CHANGE

There are constructs available that define the factors for managing complex change. There are attributes when implemented together create positive change. When any one component is missing, its absence causes the organization to fall into disarray. There are many components to plan for to become ready for change and each plan must be detailed through a PDCA process to ensure the greatest opportunity for a positive change to occur.

Definition of Readiness for Change

Being *ready for change* requires that the leader can envision that the majority of the staff will integrate the new vision. This means that staff members accept their own personal change (Reh n.d.), share in guiding beliefs, trust each other, and believe that the change will occur (Novick, Kress, and Elias 2002).

CURRENT PRACTICES THAT CONTRIBUTE
TO A READINESS FOR CHANGE PROCESS

The first step in assessing the organization's readiness for change culture is to survey stakeholders on their past experience with change and their belief in the proposed change. Using or creating online surveys such as *The Change Readiness Questionnaire* (found at www.scribd.com/doc3099867/Change-Readiness-Questionnaire) provides the organization information regarding components such as: (a) making the case for change and the vision, (b) change strategy, (c) change leadership, (d) climate of empowerment, and (e) enrollment in the change.

It is critical to create a readiness-for-change culture where "change is easily accepted and actually embraced" (Cornelius 2007, 2). Cornelius proposes four elements that will allow change to emerge and be less susceptible to resistance. These elements include stakeholders who: (a) are *business literate*, (b) feel as though they have permission to act, (c) are willing to challenge the status quo, and (d) have leaders who are willing and able to encourage a *readiness-for-change* culture.

Stakeholders who are business literate are those who understand the context of the organization and the personal impact they have on it.

> Business literacy means employees understand what the organization is trying to accomplish. They have efficacy in their work environment and know how a change in their behavior changes the performance of the organization.
> Next, stakeholders who have permission to act are those who are empowered to do so autonomously and don't have to wait for permission from supervisors.
> The third component of creating a readiness-for-change culture is having stakeholders who will challenge the status quo. They feel they are listened to and can contribute to the working conditions. This component will be further explained in the discussion in chapter 5 about *trust-to-doubt*.
> The last component is that leaders must initiate and reinforce the three aforementioned conditions. If a readiness-for-change culture is created, stakeholders will seek out, "welcome and flourish under changing conditions" (Cornelius 2007, 4). The new culture of this type of organization is continuous improvement.

COLLABORATIVE PDCA ON READINESS FOR CHANGE

In order to create a PDCA model to be ready for change, John Kotter, a professor at Harvard University, has outlined an eight-step process of creating major change (Kotter 1996, 21). Although this model is fourteen years old, the model is still valid today and is currently being used in Adams County School District 50 as the framework for the reinvention of their district.

Planning for Readiness for Change

Establishing a sense of urgency (#1), creating a guiding coalition (#2), and developing a vision and strategy (#3) (Kotter 1996) are the first three components of the planning process. The sense of systemic urgency can be created through a data-driven dialogue during a shared strategic-planning process. This involves looking at potential key performance indicators such as trends in: (a) enrollment (charter and home-schooling numbers), (b) drop-out and graduation rates, (c) proficiency on state exams, (d) attendance, and (e) satisfaction of stakeholders.

Creating the guiding coalition (Kotter 1996) helps to plan for and model the practices the organization's leadership wants everyone to emulate. In *The Tipping Point*, Malcolm Gladwell (2002) calls this coalition: mavens, connectors, and salesmen. By training a few (who understand the change, are empowered to influence others, and are supported to become a team), they will begin a grassroots effort to make the change become a reality for many.

In District 50, sixty-five teachers (two teachers in each elementary school, four in each secondary school, and one elementary pilot school) were identified to become the *beacon* teachers. Three months after the initial training of the beacons, because of the connecting and salesmen efforts of the beacon teachers to show learner-centered practices to their colleagues, another 160 teachers and instructional aides signed up to be trained, thus creating a tipping point in District 50 for the change to begin to become a part of the culture.

Another component of the planning process is ensuring all stakeholders understand the change process and their personal reaction to it. As a school begins a change process such as creating a system of *proficiency for all*, planning for the support of staff and learners through the change process is vital. When stakeholders let go of old practices (*Ending*), go through the nebulous process (*Neutral Zone*), and adopt the new practice (*New Beginning*), the change has a greater chance of success (Bridges 2003). The principalship must help people through all three stages in order for the new initiative to take hold. The phases don't happen separately and can happen simultaneously in different phases of the change.

The *Ending* begins with the transition to letting go of old practices. It requires the principalship to identify exactly what is being lost, acknowledge the losses openly, and expect stakeholders to go through the grieving process. During this time, the principalship must communicate the change by defining what's gone and what isn't. Ceremonies must be conducted to mark the ending of the old ways and allow people to take a piece of the old with them. The principalship must connect the ending with the vision of the common moral purpose and why the ending was necessary.

The *Neutral Zone* is the "no-man's-land between the old reality and the new one" (Bridges 2003, 8). This is the space where the system lets go of one trapeze bar and hasn't yet grabbed hold of the next. The dangers of the neutral zone are: (a) anxiety rises, (b) people miss more work, (c) weaknesses become worse, (d) people lose their confidence, (e) polarization happens, as some want to go back and some move forward, and (f) the organization or school is vulnerable to attack.

However, the neutral zone is a time to encourage innovation. The school needs to create new temporary systems, such as setting short-range goals and strengthening connections within the school, to use during the neutral zone. This is a time to question current practices that may not work in the new system and encourage experimentation. This is a productive time and should not be moved through too quickly (Bridges 2003).

The *New Beginning* is the expression of the new identity for the school. To launch it appropriately, the principalship must be able to explain the basic purpose, paint a picture of the new change, share the plan, and give each person a part to play in the new beginning. During this time, it is important to: (a) be consistent, (b) ensure and celebrate quick successes, and (c) symbolize the new identity (Bridges 2003).

Developing a vision and a strategy (Kotter 1996) is the final component of the planning process. In order to enroll stakeholders in creating a plan that will achieve the strategies to make their vision become a reality, staff should know the stakeholders, speak to them about a future that serves their interests, and invite them to dream of a better system (Kouzes and Posner 2006).

Being Ready for Change

The remaining steps in Kotter's model will not be accomplished until the change is activated. However, in Readiness for Change, planning for these steps is crucial. Planning must be done in Kotter's (1996) areas of communicating the change (#4), empowering broad-based action (#5), and how the organization will generate short-term wins (#6).

Creating plans concerning how all stakeholders will be informed about the change and receive answers to their questions involves face-to-face conversations, internal print media, public media outlets, an interactive website, and informing learners so they can be the ambassadors for the change.

Before starting broad-based action, members of the organization should ensure there is ownership of the change. This means reaching consensus about moving forward with the change or determining what is still needed. In District 50, they took a vote of confidence after six months of building awareness and a skill set about this philosophy. They received an 85 percent affirmative vote to pursue becoming a learner-centric, standards-driven school district.

Empowering broad-based action involves identifying and eliminating barriers to the implementation of the change. A systems audit will need to be conducted to determine what systems and procedures will remain and which will be adapted or removed. Schedules, grading, report cards, and evaluation rubrics are just some structures District 50 has modified as they transition to a learner-centric, standards-driven system. Using the guiding coalition to take risks and give feedback on what practices are working for them and what systems need to redesigned or abandoned support the empowerment of the staff.

Planning for short-term wins means identifying the baseline results and setting goals and cycle times for the expected gains. The system needs to benchmark periodically to ensure these wins and plan for the recognition of the members of the staff who make the wins possible.

Checking and Adjusting Readiness for Change

The organization needs to plan for the consolidation of the gains and production of more change (#7) (Kotter 1996). This involves checking KPIs on predetermined cycle times and adjusting plans accordingly. Doug Reeves (2002) has created a matrix that demonstrates how leaders must understand why they are doing what they are doing and if the actions are connected to improving results. This tool can then be used to determine whether a practice should be replicated or should be abandoned. This may mean changes to classroom practice and district policies and procedures. It should be used collaboratively with the principalship, teachers, and learners. It is important that all stakeholders understand the leverage points that lead to improved results.

To create a system aligned to the vision, the recruitment of staff, an effective induction program of new families and staff, and an ongoing targeted professional-development plan based on observations and learner results will support the creation and sustainability of the system. This provides for coherence-making and knowledge-creation and sharing (Fullan 2001, 4).

Kotter completes his model with step #8: anchoring new approaches in the culture. Planning for this step means the planning for sustainability and the ownership of the change. This means having PDCA plans and measures that show improvement and anchoring them to the new changes. The communication and celebration of this improvement and its connection to the changes is critical and motivates stakeholders to continuously improve. A crucial step at this time is ensuring the succession planning for leadership in critical positions to ensure the vision is sustainable.

Once the system is ready to change, the stakeholders must ensure that they have a trusting environment because "trust allows change to occur" (Novick, Kress, and Elias 2002, 1). Chapter 5 deals with creating a *trust-to-doubt* process so stakeholders will trust one another enough to question current practices.

Table 4.1. Creating the Culture of Readiness-for-Change Continua

	Category	Beginning School	Developing School	Proficient School	Advanced School Meets All Proficient Criteria, Plus
PLAN	Developing a sense of urgency	• Doesn't know how to use data to identify issues or improve practice.	• Uses summative data to track progress and data begins to create a sense of urgency in individual teacher/learner.	• Uses data-driven dialogue process on data as it's generated. • Uses formative and summative data to create a sense of urgency.	• Uses data-driven dialogue process with multiple-year trend data. • Uses formative and summative data regularly to create a culture of continuous improvement.
	Building a guiding coalition of staff and learners	• Sees no need to change. • Allows external factors of school community to paralyze motivation.	• Begins to understand that staff and learners have control to make a difference during the school day.	• Feels empowered to embrace change and learn new skills. • Develops a culture of transparency with new skills. • Sets up a process to solve problems. • Identifies a structure for others to see practice.	• Understands that *proficiency for all* requires a new set of skills, knowledge, tools, and processes to accomplish its goal and documents practices and shares with others.
	Developing knowledge and skill set in change process	• Doesn't plan for development of prerequisite skills and knowledge for staff and learner to be ready for change.	• Assesses skills and knowledge of staff on readiness for change to determine individual and school-wide needs. • Develops and deploys knowledge and skill set in: Understands change process	• Uses knowledge and skill set to create processes to assist stakeholders in understanding need for change. • Checks for accurate deployment of knowledge and skill set by identifying KPIs.	• Uses knowledge and skill set to understand that change is inevitable and will be necessary to allow for continuous improvement.

(continued)

Table 4.1. (*continued*)

	Category	Beginning School	Developing School	Proficient School	Advanced School Meets All Proficient Criteria, Plus
PLAN			• Understands implication of change on stakeholders Understands implementation dip Disaggregates data to create a sense of urgency Understands internal and external locus of control	• Creates trainings for new staff and learners annually in change process.	
	Recruiting staff	• Doesn't address readiness for change in recruiting or hiring process.	• Hires for an openness to new ideas.	• Hires for a reflective practice. • Recruits staff with skill set for creating a culture for change process.	• Creates sustainability through recruiting and professional development to ensure a culture for change.
DO	Creating a communication plan for change	• Doesn't have a communication plan change processes. • Doesn't plan to use the guiding coalition to communicate to rest of the staff.	• Uses word-of-mouth communication vehicles to communicate the change. • Uses the guiding coalition in a limited manner to communicate to others. • Doesn't have feedback loops in place to respond to questions.	• Plans to use written and oral conduits to communicate the vision. • Uses the guiding coalition to model the prospective change. • Has a multipronged approach to two-way communication with stakeholders.	• Uses media, the web to communicate the vision and strategies. • Uses the guiding coalition to train colleagues for the prospective change.

DO	Empowering broad-based action	• Doesn't monitor readiness-for-change process.	• Supports change with a "one size fits all" model.	• Analyzes level of change for each individual stakeholder and provides reason and support for emotional and cognitive growth.	• Assists stakeholders in connecting their efficacy in change to positive learner achievement.
	Involving learners	• Doesn't involve learners in change process.	• Involves learner leadership in change process. • Seeks input, but not involvement.	• Creates a two-way communication plan for learners. • Creates a skill set for change in learners. • Creates learner working groups to plan for change.	• Creates a venue for all learners to identify problems and create solutions.
	Owning the change	• Doesn't have a process to check to see if staff is ready for change.	• Checks with small groups of staff to determine readiness for change.	• Has formal process to determine readiness for change for entire staff (e.g., vote of confidence).	• Has a process for staff-initiated change suggestions. • Uses change process independently to solve problems.
	Celebrating short-term wins	• Doesn't have a celebration process.	• Doesn't celebrate short-term wins in a timely manner.	• Celebrates KPIs from a formative benchmark internally.	• Celebrates KPIs from a formative benchmark externally to all stakeholders.

(continued)

Table 4.1. *(continued)*

	Category	Beginning School	Developing School	Proficient School	Advanced School Meets All Proficient Criteria, Plus
CHECK	Analyzing KPIs on cycle times	• Defends status quo. • Has no cycle time to evaluate data.	• Evaluates KPIs on an *annual* cycle.	• Evaluates KPIs on a *semester* cycle.	• Evaluates KPIs on a *quarterly* or *monthly* cycle.
CHECK	Improving continuously	• Doesn't analyze a state of readiness or know how to prepare stakeholders to be ready for a change initiative.	• Plans for resiliency through the implementation dip. • Plans for stakeholder resistance or apathy with a new initiative.	• Analyzes gap between current state and being ready for change initiative. • Expands coalitions to move staff and learners from current state to readiness. • Adjusts practice based on continuous improvement cycle.	• Prepares and shares detailed plans for readiness process with all schools in district to be ready for a change initiative. • Adjusts practice for sustained change through multiple continuous improvement cycles for deep implementation.
ADJUST	Refining based on checking process	• Doesn't adjust practice based on KPIs.	• Begins to evaluate practices based on KPIs.	• Adjusts practices based on results of KPIs, if necessary.	• Adjusts practices in line with data collection on more frequent cycle times, if necessary.

ADJUST				
Anchoring the new approaches in the culture	• Has "silo-ed" change activities in each building so there is no sharing. • No policy review in light of change initiative. • No data collection on change initiative.	• Has asynchronous process for reviewing policies and procedures in light of the change. • Has an ineffective method of data collection aligned to the change initiative.	• Creates a systematic process of policy and procedure alignment. • Connects qualitative and quantitative data to the change initiative. • Shows change initiative had a positive impact on learner achievement.	• Plans to share successful change initiatives that show increased learner achievement. • Plans for succession planning for leadership.
Creating rituals and ceremonies of a change culture	• Doesn't celebrate rituals to acknowledge readiness.	• Does not match magnitude of celebration to magnitude of change.	• Celebrates that internal stakeholders are ready for change.	• Creates ceremonies with all stakeholders to mark being ready to start change initiative.

Suggested evidences:
➤ Data that documents a sense of urgency
➤ PDCA plans with KPIs and cycle times to monitor change readiness
➤ Plans that begin with the end in mind
➤ Evidence of celebrations
➤ List of activities from the guiding coalition
➤ Communication plan
➤ School-improvement plan

➤ Assessment of the readiness-for-change: staff, parents, and learners
➤ Recruitment and professional development plans for creation of a culture for the change process.
➤ Learner involvement in the readiness for change
➤ Data used to identify problems and create plans for solutions
➤ List of staff for whom change is first and second order and plans to support their personal transition

READINESS FOR CHANGE:
CONVERSATIONS WITH THE STAKEHOLDERS

Voices of the Principals

Question: "How do you create a sense of urgency?" Principals all responded that they used data-digs. Previously, Chris Benisch and Kelly Williams emphasized that because they had not made any significant or systemic change, they could almost predict their state annual scores. Williams came to the realization that what they were doing wasn't working. She was blunt in sharing her scores with her staff. She said, "With the results we have, it isn't that hard to create that urgency for change. We all know we need to change."

Benisch added that the key was "that everything from central office down [which was changing] made everybody go 'WOW, we really are going to do something.'" . . . This wasn't just a program we were going to buy and send people to. Sarah Gould expounded that we now have tools to sustain a systemic change. We're able to go back to our shared vision, the OSAT (RISC's Organizational Self-Assessment Tool), everyone has tools to sustain a sense of urgency.

Knowing that staff would be going through second-order change, principals were asked how they have supported staff and students through the change process. Bill Stuckey, principal at Shaw Heights Middle School, and Gould emphasized the power of relationships. They both detailed that knowing what was going on in classrooms and with teachers supported this course of action. Benisch expanded that he needed to provide resources and release his power and control, "doing less officiating," and trust his staff to be the experts.

Williams concluded that it was important for staff and students to feel they had permission to make mistakes in this system. Using the "check and adjust" process helps refine the implementation. She feels the transition has been harder on the teachers. For her it doesn't even feel like a change. She said, "It feels like we are going toward the light."

Voices of the Teachers

Question: "How have you opened up yourself to look at data, analyze root causes and adjust your practice?" The main theme was keeping the focus on the student and their learning. Robin Kietzmann said she used a data dialogue with her third-graders when they looked at what they missed on their tests, and she told her students it's not about "'feeling bad,' it's about what do you need to know." Jennifer Rizzo followed up that she has taught her students to use data to become better learners. "It's not about failing/passing, it's about how does it help you know more about yourself as a learner and what your needs are."

Teachers felt that they needed to be ready for change on a personal and collaborative level. Greg Russo responded that giving up the control is the best thing for you as the teacher and the students: "It's hugely beneficial for both. If I can still understand, it's not giving up control and not teaching anymore, it's changing how you are teaching."

Anne Marie Dadley stated she has been ready for this change since she became a teacher. A student working toward being proficient and not working for grades "is what I got into teaching for."

Janelle Stastny has been sharing some of her practices with other teachers. When sharing a rubric with others, her colleagues said they would need to change it because their students wouldn't be successful, and that they would have to bring it down. Stastny reported saying, "No, standards are standards!" It will be a change for some teachers to scaffold their students' learning up to the standards.

Voices of the Learners

Question: "What changes have you experienced this year?" The students focused on three main themes: (a) working at their own pace, (b) learning from one another, and (c) perceiving that their teachers cared more about their learning. Anna explained that she liked working at her own pace because she "didn't have to do assignments over and over again until the class got it right."

Maria (a pseudonym) said that she learned more working in centers because the teacher would explain what to do and the students would then work together. Penny concurred that "When we help one another, we learn more by each other. We can talk about it and hear the other person's ideas and make up a real good answer for it."

Anna feels her teacher cares more about her learning this year. She said, "Teachers actually care this year, instead of just letting us work by ourselves. Last year they told you once and you'd have to do it and left you to your own devices. They didn't care if you got it right or not."

Voices of the Parents

Question: "How is the school was preparing you for change?" All four parents reported that they felt the school staff was trying to do more. Tomasita said that her child's school was "trying to do more by sending home newsletters on Friday and trying to call us one-on-one. It's a lot better."

Jason, whose child goes to another district school, concurs that the school personnel communicates with him about these changes through a weekly newsletter, follow-up phone calls once a week, and e-mail. They "try to close the loop on communication." Danielle felt the school's invitation to a seminar on standards-based awareness helped her understand better but it was still pretty new.

Key Points in Chapter 4:

1. How do you plan for a change culture?

   The principalship must create a PDCA to move each stakeholder to a culture of change through a series of steps such as Kotter's Leading Change model. Principals need to plan to support individual transitions through Bridges' stages of change: the Ending, the Neutral Zone, and the New Beginning.

2. How does creating a culture of change prepare the adults for the twenty-first-century skills the students will need to learn?

   American educators have been educated, trained as educators, and now work in a system that has changed little in their lifetime. These skills have served them in the past but will not help them be successful in the future. Educators must learn a new set of tools and processes to engage the learner, adapt to change, and teach what will be expected in the twenty-first century.

Creating the Culture of Trust-to-Doubt

Fundamental components of chapter 5:

- Current Practices that Show Need for Trust-to-Doubt
- Combining Trust and Doubt
- Current Practices that Contribute to a Trust-to-Doubt Process
- How to Create a Trust-to-Doubt Process
- Creating the Culture of Trust-to-Doubt Continua
- Trust-to-Doubt: Conversations with Stakeholders
- Key Points in Chapter 5

Guiding Questions in Chapter 5:

1. What are the philosophical and historical premises of combining trust with the doubting process?
2. Why would you need a trust-to-doubt process and how would you create the process?

CURRENT PRACTICES THAT SHOW
NEED FOR TRUST-TO-DOUBT

In chapter 1, low and stagnant scores from a district, state, and national perspective were acknowledged. The current educational system, in a time of increased expectations and accountability, is not yielding the *proficiency-for-all* results desired and yet very little is being done to change the system. Many are making superficial changes but few are making the systemic changes needed to meet the needs of the current learner population and twenty-first-century societal needs. Our current educational practices must be challenged and schools will need to engage in a process to make this come to fruition.

In many districts and schools in our nation, trust has been waning. Too often initiatives are thrust upon staff with little continuous vision and support for new skills. The lack of vision causes staff to be frustrated and the lack of skill development causes the new initiative to grow at glacial speed. Thus, new initiatives show little or no impact and are abandoned (York-Barr et al. 2001).

This leaves veteran staff to wait out the current *initiative du jour*, because in their experience this will pass, only to be replaced by the next fad. Because this is the pattern, the staff lacks trust that any reform will improve achievement. Our schools have cultures that *doubt-to-trust* and must be transformed into ones that will *trust-to-doubt*.

The need to align educational practice to a common moral purpose, *proficiency for all* and twenty-first-century skills, will require all stakeholders to call into question firmly entrenched school practices and policies. The authors have crafted a process to guide this questioning that is called creating a culture of *trust-to-doubt*. With the culture of *trust-to-doubt* in place, restructuring efforts will focus on creating a system that will achieve *proficiency for all* and will make these efforts sustainable.

Hence, an effective *trust-to-doubt* process should be used to focus reform efforts with the expectation of creating a culture where the staff will question itself and allow for continuous improvement. This will help learners gain the skills and knowledge to proficiency that would enable them to be successful in their future.

Challenging Mental Models

The challenging of the public's and staff's mental model of public education will be one of the toughest hurdles to overcome. Mental models (Senge 1990, 8) are "deeply ingrained assumptions, generalizations, pictures or images that influence how we understand the world and how we take action." These assumptions concerning public education are not easily abandoned and replaced when faced with conflicting information.

Most people have a picture of public education from when they were in school. These mental models were constructed when there was only an expectation of *proficiency for some*. Educators now have data and research to show that our current educational system is not reaching the expectation of *proficiency for all*, so the same model of school will not be sufficient to accomplish this goal.

Definition of Trust

Trust is defined as social trust, and within that realm, relational trust is the "calculation whereby an individual decides whether or not to engage in an action with another individual that incorporates some degree of risk" (Bryk and Schneider 2002, 14). In order to build trust (York-Barr et al. 2001, 24–26), one must:

(a) be present and aware,
(b) be open,
(c) listen without judgment and with empathy,
(d) seek understanding (Covey, as cited in York-Barr et al. [2001]),
(e) view learning as mutual, and
(f) honor the person and the process.

Individuals build trust by discerning positive intentions through the lens of respect, competence, personal regard for others, and integrity (Bryk and Schneider 2002).

In schools, trust is defined as a mutual dependency among all the key actors, which is regularly validated by consistent actions. A break in trust occurs when expectations are not met, leading to a weakening of relationships and in more extreme situations, a severing of ties. The strength of relational trust is validated through looking at the behaviors and examining the perceived intentions of the individual. Barbara Bryk and Tony Schneider's conclusions about trust are "where high levels of social trust exist, cooperative efforts for improvement should be easier to initiate and sustain" (Bryk and Schneider 2002, 13).

Definition of "Doubt" and "Doubting Process"

Doubt is defined as "an inquiry into routine and habitual perceptions and assumptions that are generally conceived as appropriate within some social system of values and beliefs" (Schechter 2006, 2475). Schechter also defines the *doubting process* as the "ethical and productive inducement of doubt in light of the versatile, dynamic, and contextual conditions of an organization, which, then, contributes to its effective use" (Schechter 2006, 2475).

In a continuous improvement process, it's vital for the stakeholders to be able to doubt current practices in order to improve them for the future. Historically, doubt was perceived in a positive light through cynics and skeptics doubting their current assumptions and creating new scientific, analytical processes to establish truth. Recently, in popular culture, doubt has been perceived more negatively. When a person says they doubt something, they really mean it is unlikely to be or happen. The authors would contend that doubt, in its original form, is a necessary process in continuous improvement.

COMBINING TRUST AND DOUBT

In order for significant reform to occur in school, staff must engage in creating a trusting environment before beginning a doubting process. When beginning a *trust-to-doubt* process, staff should begin with issues that are less emotional in order to build trust in the process and among the participants. "In high–trust cultures, collective decision-making with broad teacher buy-in occurs more readily, reform initiatives are more likely to be deeply engaged by school participants, and it stimulates a moral imperative to take on the hard work of school improvement" (Bryk and Schneider 2002, 122–23).

This process cannot be initiated from the top (Schechter 2006). If this discussion comes only from leadership, there will be resistance to change and thus little chance for the practitioners and their partners (learners) to trust the results of a doubting process (Schechter 2006). It confounds stakeholders' sense of control and increases the possibility of withdrawal from the situation.

This is not to say that district and central-office support is not crucial to establishing the conditions for *trust-to-doubt* to occur. Indeed, it is essential that all stakeholders make this journey together. "Doubting the organization's ongoing practices increases the burden and responsibilities of all its stakeholders yet at the same time, it evokes the organization's tremendous potential for individual and communal growth" (Schechter 2006, 2477). To summarize, combining trust and doubt, the authors adapted Descartes' famous quote, "I think, therefore I am" to "We trust and doubt, therefore we learn and grow."

CURRENT PRACTICES THAT CONTRIBUTE
TO A TRUST-TO-DOUBT PROCESS

Professional Learning Community, Collaborative Inquiry,
and Reflective Practice

Currently there are components of a *trust-to-doubt* process in use but no one has packaged these processes together with the outcome being *proficiency for all* learners. Professional Learning Communities (PLCs) require staff to:

(a) create a shared mission,
(b) participate in collective inquiry through gathering and analyzing data,
(c) meet in collaborative teams,
(d) become action-oriented,
(e) commit to continuous improvement through never being satisfied with the status quo, and
(f) orient toward results (DuFour and Eaker 1998, 25–29).

Trust-to-doubt is actionable in PLCs through shared mission and collaborative teams being based on trust and collective inquiry and lack of satisfaction with the status quo reinforcing the doubting process.

Collaborative inquiry (Love et al. 2008) defines the process for schools to continuously improve practice. "It investigates the current status of student learning and instructional practice and searches for successes to celebrate and amplify" (Love et al. 2008, 18). Critical elements of a high-performing data culture include:

(a) leadership and capacity,
(b) collaboration,
(c) data use,
(d) instructional improvement,
(e) equity, and
(f) trust.

The common themes between PLCs and collaborative inquiry are that trust is built through collaboration, equity, and trust-building, and doubt is reinforced through use of data and looking for instructional improvement.

Reflective practice (York-Barr et al. 2001, 7) is an inquiry approach to teaching that involves a personal commitment to continuous learning and improvement. It currently is defined as:

(a) deliberate pause;
(b) open perspective;
(c) thinking processes;
(d) examination of beliefs, goals, and practices;
(e) new insights and understandings; and
(f) actions that improve learning.

This adds having an open perspective to the trust and thinking processes, examining beliefs, gaining new insights, and improving learning to the doubting process.

While all of these constructs encourage increased achievement, none of them involve learners in their processes nor set a goal of *proficiency for all*. They discuss teacher practices but do not discuss the role that learners play in becoming partners in any inquiry. The doubting process questions all practices within the school, celebrates effective procedures, and aligns all processes with the shared vision, while eliminating ineffective modes of operation.

HOW TO CREATE A TRUST-TO-DOUBT PROCESS

To unleash the power of a culture of *trust-to-doubt* at least three things must occur (Schechter 2006):

> Stakeholders, including the learners, must feel a need for change (Schechter 2006). Our current system hasn't been structured to ensure *proficiency for all* (Stiggins 2008). Mediocre results must be highlighted to all stakeholders from our current practice, in order for them to understand the need for change.

> All stakeholders must have the opportunity to discuss the reasons for the necessity of creating a *trust-to-doubt* process (Schechter 2006). Determining a process to look at the current results of an initiative, determining the root causes for those results, and questioning the effectiveness of current practice must be a component of the doubting process. If there is a built-in process in the system through a PDCA, the doubting process is a component of the *checking* phase.

> When planning for a *trust-to-doubt* culture, allowance must be made for intellectual and emotional responses (Schechter 2006). Our schools are full of stakeholders who are human. John Dewey (1909, as cited in Schechter [2006]) noted that the key for ethical knowledge is the understanding of emotional responsiveness. Humans will not engage in the risky process of challenging current practice unless the climate encourages them, without sanction. Thus, emotional safety becomes a major factor in establishing an effective *trust-to-doubt* culture. That safety, which will assure constructive, active participation in a doubting process, must be anchored in trust (Schechter 2006).

Collaborative PDCA on Trust-to-Doubt

In order to establish a systemic implementation of a collaborative trust-to-doubt process, teachers and principals must collaborate on a PDCA format. Each step of the process is outlined below:

1) In the *planning* phase, the staff and learners must be prepared for readiness to trust by building a culture that aligns actions to beliefs. This will build trust throughout the system. A knowledge and skill set in the doubting process must be developed in the principalship and the staff through recruitment and professional development. Plans for sustainability and systems thinking must include seeking root causes through data analysis, determining leverage points, and setting action plans and cycle times for review.

2) The action plans encompass the *doing* phase of implementing a doubting process. It is important to realize that this is a very human process so the integration of intellect and emotion into this process is critical. Staff will be using new doubting tools and processes to examine their own and the organization's mental models. These tools and processes include:

   (a) *plus/delta charts* to give feedback on lessons, meetings, and processes;
   (b) *5 Whys* to determine root causes; and
   (c) the *Bone diagram* to assist in the identification of issues in the current situation, the desired state, and the forces that will drive and restrain progress (www.asq.org). This may cause stress and change in the organization and the principalship must manage staff's reaction during the change process.

3) In the creation of action plans, it is essential that the plans are *checked* at certain intervals for progress. Key performance indicators must be benchmarked against the goals set. Shortened cycle times will increase responsiveness of the system.

4) After the key performance indicators are checked, adjustments to action plans must be made after results are deemed on- or off-track. Continuous improvement will occur as the results hone in on the goal. Celebrations of this process will motivate staff to stay focused on the process.

It is important to note that maintaining trust for a doubting process must be an ongoing practice, not an episode. Stakeholders require regular updates on the results of changes from the *trust-to-doubt* process to make it relevant. The reader will note how important this is by reviewing the continua that follow this narrative. "For relational trust to develop and sustain, adults and students must make sense of their work together in terms of what they understand as the primary purpose of the public school" (Bryk and Schneider 2002, 136–37)). This leads to exploring ideas about collective efficacy in chapter 6.

Table 5.1. Creating the Culture of Trust-to-Doubt Process Continua

Categories	Beginning School	Developing School	Proficient School	Advanced School Meets All Proficient Criteria, Plus
Preparing stakeholders for trust-to-doubt process	• Doesn't allow stakeholders to doubt any processes or disagree with current practice for fear of humiliation or reprisal.	• Determines root causes of trust/distrust. • Looks for leverage points to improve trust. • Explains definition of trust and doubt. • Experiments with a doubting process on safe issues.	• Creates a trusting climate for an internal process of doubt to occur on all issues.	• Doubting process becomes a "way of doing business." • Invites external stakeholders to contribute to doubting process.

Developing a knowledge and skill set	• Doesn't seek out professional development and learning opportunities about trust building and doubting process.	• Assesses skills and knowledge of staff on trust and doubt to determine individual and school-wide needs.
		• Develop and deploy knowledge and skill set in:
		  Developing norms and protocols for building trust and doubting process;
		  Engaging staff intellectually and emotionally; and
			• Models a trust-to-doubt process through questions, protocols, and meetings to improve school culture and learning.
			• Manages personal transitions in change process for staff and learners (second-order change).
			• Checks for accurate deployment of knowledge and skill set based on identifying KPIs.
				• Creates ongoing professional development to ensure continuation of a culture for the trust-to-doubt process.

PLAN

PDCA Phase	Element				
PLAN					
	Creating a trust-to-doubt culture to improve achievement	• Doesn't monitor trust-to-doubt process.	• Begins to create a process of doubt using only safe issues. • Little to no connection of doubting process to achievement.	Understanding mental models concerning learner-centric, standards-driven environments. • Uses a doubting process in a safe environment by modeling through questions, protocols, and meetings. • Trains new staff and learners annually in trust-to-doubt. • Analyzes data on a regular basis to determine goals and ensures stakeholders have established a trusting relationship and are ready to engage in doubting process. • Uses trust-to-doubt process to improve practice, which is reflected in achievement.	• Is seen as model of trust-to-doubt process to emulate based on trend data.
	Recruiting staff	• Doesn't address trust-to-doubt process in recruiting or hiring process.	• Hires for an openness to new ideas.	• Creates a plan to hire for a reflective practice philosophy. • Recruits staff with skill set for creating a culture for trust-to-doubt process.	• Creates sustainability through refining the criteria for recruitment of staff who are open to a trust-to-doubt process.
DO	Integrating intellect and emotion into trust-to-doubt process	• Has no formal process for trust-to-doubt process to occur, and manifests itself by no one confronting issues productively.	• Creates a limited venue (intellectual issues) to begin to use trust-to-doubt process.	• Uses data for a productive use of trust-to-doubt process and problem solving.	• Integrates both intellect and emotion as necessary forces for a productive use of trust-to-doubt process.

(continued)

Table 5.1. (continued)

	Categories	Beginning School	Developing School	Proficient School	Advanced School Meets All Proficient Criteria, Plus
DO	Analyzing mental models	• Doesn't question themselves ("It's the way we've always done it").	• Begins to uncover mental models under which stakeholders operate.	• Makes stakeholders' mental models transparent on all issues.	• Questions mental models of their organizational behavior and individual stakeholders' mental models.
	Managing change during doubting process	• Feels criticized or incompetent during any trust-to-doubt process.	• Supports one another in building capacity during trust-to-doubt process.	• Manages personal change in competency and efficacy when trust-to-doubt process occurs.	• Invokes doubting process when conflict occurs between common moral purpose and a current practice. • Researches problems and synthesizes solutions back into system.
	Involving learners	• Doesn't involve learners in trust-to-doubt process.	• Involves learner leadership in trust-to-doubt process. • Seeks their input, but not involvement.	• Creates a process for all learners to contribute to trust-to-doubt process, creates working groups to plan for a change in practice.	• Creates a venue for all learners to doubt current practice and create solutions.
CHECK	Analyzing KPIs on cycle times	• Defends status quo. • Has no cycle times to evaluate data.	• Implements a trust-to-doubt to analyze KPIs on an *annual* cycle.	• Implements a trust-to-doubt process to analyze KPIs on a cycle or pre-determined times.	• Implements a trust-to-doubt process to analyze KPIs on an accelerated basis.

ADJUST				
Refining based on checking process	Doesn't adjust practice based on KPI review.	Begins to evaluate practices based on KPIs.	Adjusts practices based on results of KPIs.	Adjusts practices in line with data collection on more frequent cycle times.
Improving continuously	Doesn't want to "rock the boat" or create cognitive dissonance in stakeholders.	Begins to "plant seeds of doubt" using data or reflective questions.	Evokes organization's potential for individual and common growth.	Creates a continuous process of trust-to-doubt as the underlying force for further inquiry, which is never satisfied with results obtained.
Celebrating	Celebrates status quo (no doubt occurred).	Seeks out stakeholders to ask "doubting" questions so that trust-to-doubt can be positively reinforced.	Creates a positive environment when trust-to-doubt process is undertaken. Reinforces (positively) stakeholders who take the risk to doubt current practices.	Celebrates trust-to-doubt process when it achieves positive results or even when it doesn't.

Suggested evidences:

➤ Set of written norms for groups
➤ Create a PDCA plan for developing a trust-to doubt process with KPI's and cycle times
➤ Trust-to-doubt process protocol in the classroom or school
➤ Agenda of trust-to-doubt process meetings that highlight uncovering biases/mental models
➤ Decision-making matrix
➤ Defines and schedules the trust-to-doubt process on regular cycles or when needed
➤ Recruitment and professional development plan
➤ Agenda of use of protocols
➤ Plan for managing second order change
➤ Evidence of celebration of trust-to-doubt process
➤ Evidence of data used to support the continuation or elimination of a practice

TRUST-TO-DOUBT:
CONVERSATIONS WITH THE STAKEHOLDERS

Voices of the Principals

Question: "What have you done to build trust during this time of change?" All the principals agreed that to have a culture where you trust-to-doubt, you have to build relational trust. Bill Stuckey discussed that if you build relationships with people they will go out on a limb and try new things. This will allow people to struggle and know you won't come down on them. To build relationships you must be visible, have informal conversations, be in hallways, and get to know them and let them get to know you.

Sarah Gould says that it's important to reinforce staff's comfort with ambiguity during these drastic times of change. She uses her relationship with staff to allow them to meltdown when they need to and that it's okay not to have all the answers. The staff has to come up with the answers together.

Chris Benisch says a principal must release control, put your power in your pocket, but define what you need and give the staff control to get it done. His staff has used Judith Warren Little's *continuum of collegiality* to make relationships more transparent. They have unpacked each placement on the continuum and given each other permission to confront one another by saying, "you need to reframe that."

Kelly Williams reemphasized the need for an alignment between the beliefs and behaviors through the shared vision. She felt she demonstrated this when she walked the talk between her own personal beliefs and behaviors. Benisch believes that through developing the shared vision, staff is building trust. They support each other 100 percent, share ideas, disagree safely, and give critical feedback. His staff is now bringing student work to share with one another not just successes—when it bombs, they ask for help from colleagues.

In order to doubt current practices and identify areas that no longer align in a standards-driven environment, principals reported using tools and a PDCA process to refine their continuous improvement. Williams and Stuckey reported using a parking lot, "5 Whys," and a data-driven dialogue to solve achievement and issues as they arise in the building. Gould and Williams describe their PDCA process as they worked on discipline issues, Response to Intervention (RtI), and adjustment to a new school.

Voices of the Teachers

Question: What have you done to build trust during this time of change? Janelle Stastny said that teachers need to let go of egos and come together like first-year teachers. This is a whole new way of teaching. We need to help each other relearn how to teach. This needs to happen in a trusting atmosphere so we can have a common atmosphere. It's not all about us. We have come together to ensure our students' success across the board. We have a lot of discussions about what is working for us and what isn't working for us. The classroom teaching that I used to do, like whole class instruction, doesn't fit anymore. Some kids aren't ready to move on, while others are. You need to understand the lecture approach won't work for everyone.

Question: What practices have been doubted? Stastny explained that in her school, vertical teams have given a venue to share teaching strategies which have doubted some teaching practices. "It has shown what's working and what is not and now the difference is I can admit that what I was doing wasn't effective for some kids and come to the team for help."

Voices of the Learners

Question: "Do you have a good relationship with your teacher so you can tell them when things are working/ not working for you?" All learners responded with a resounding "Yes!" Anna described their classes' input process. She said, "We have this chart at school, teacher leaves the room, we describe what went well, what needs to be improved, what questions you have. We put our ideas on a stickee note." She described that the teacher would reenter the room and answer the questions and often does what the students ask.

She stated that last year the teacher "ignored us and did it her way." This year she knows her teacher cares and she will help her on that subject. Penny added in her class, "We sit in our groups in a meeting and we talk and the teacher will do something about it."

Voices of the Parents

Question: "If you see a practice that doesn't align with the shared vision of Standards-based System (SBS), what avenues do you have available to express your opinion?" Parents responded that they have several avenues to express their opinion if they questioned the procedures of the school. Joseph Maldonado and Jason Reynolds both said they would start with the teacher and use e-mail and phone calls, then go to the principal if needed.

With this new direction that their children have experienced, all the parents unanimously agreed that they trust that the school is going in the right direction. They emphasized that they must stay involved in their children's education to ensure their children stay on track and graduate on time.

Key Points in Chapter 5:

1. What are the philosophical and historical premises of combining trust with the doubting process?

   Relational trust is the extent to which people decide to engage in a risky action with another person. The doubting process is an avenue to doubt current practices in order to improve. Historically, doubt was perceived as necessary to challenge current assumptions to establish truth. Currently, the concept of doubt has taken on a more negative tone, because people take doubt personally, instead of focusing doubting on the action. By combining trust and doubt, stakeholders are invited to give feedback in a safe environment for improvement.

2. Why would you need a trust-to-doubt process and how would you create the process?

   For an effective PDCA cycle for trust-to-doubt, stakeholders must provide honest feedback on results and be able to examine the causes and adjust practices without repercussions. This must be ongoing and continued to be tied to the common moral purpose.

· *6* ·

Creating the Culture of
Learner-Centric, Collective Efficacy

Fundamental components of chapter 6:

- Current Practices That Show Need for Collective Efficacy
- Current Practices That Contribute to Collective Efficacy
- Creating a PDCA for Learner-Centric Collective Efficacy
- Creating the Culture of Learner-Centric Collective Efficacy Continua
- Learner-Centric Collective Efficacy: Conversations with Stakeholders
- Key Points in Chapter 6

Guiding Questions in Chapter 6:

1. What is the difference between teacher and collective efficacy for a school staff?
2. Why did the authors coin the term "learner-centric collective efficacy"?
3. How do you build learner-centric collective efficacy within a school culture?

CURRENT PRACTICES THAT SHOW
NEED FOR COLLECTIVE EFFICACY

A review of the literature finds research on self-efficacy, individual teacher efficacy, and collective adult efficacy in a school, but reveals neglect of the role of learners in creating collective efficacy (Goddard 2003; Hoy, Smith, and Sweetland 2002). According to Roger Goddard, Wayne Hoy, and Anita Woolfolk Hoy (2004, 3): "Researchers have found links between achievement and three kinds of efficacy:

(a) the self-efficacy judgments of students (Pajares [1994, 1997], as cited in Goddard, Hoy, and Hoy [2004]),
(b) teachers' beliefs in their own instructional efficacy (Tschannen-Moran et al. [1998], as cited in Goddard, Hoy, and Hoy [2004]); and
(c) teachers' beliefs about the collective efficacy of their school" (Goddard, Hoy, and Woolfolk Hoy [2000], as cited in Goddard, Hoy, and Hoy [2004]).

No one has included learners as participants when examining the impact of collective efficacy of the school. Further research must be done on this concept both in teacher-directed and learner-centric classrooms.

Definition of Teacher Efficacy

Self-efficacy is a perceived judgment about a specific task capability. Teacher efficacy is the perception of competence versus actual competence or performance in the classroom. It does not connote effectiveness. However, Goddard, Hoy, and Hoy (2004) cited that teachers with strong perceptions of capability tend to "employ classroom strategies that are more organized and better planned (Allinder 1994), student-centered (Czerniak and Schriver 1994, Enochs, Scharmann and Riggs 1995), and humanistic (Woolfolk and Hoy, 1990)."

Definition of Collective Efficacy

Collective efficacy in schools is the "shared perceptions of teachers in a school that the efforts of the faculty as a whole will have positive effects on students" (Hoy 2009, 1). All efficacy beliefs, no matter who holds these beliefs, are future-oriented about capabilities to create a course of action to accomplish a goal (Bandura [1997], as cited in Goddard, Hoy, and Hoy [2004]). Goddard, Hoy, and Hoy (2004) describe the issue as "Can I (the student or teacher) or we (the faculty) orchestrate the thoughts and actions to perform the task?" The authors would contend that the *we* should be the *faculty and learners* building collective efficacy together.

The authors' new definition of collective efficacy in a school is *the shared perceptions of teacher and Learners in a school that the efforts of the faculty and Learners as a whole will have a positive effect on the learning.* This is supported by the recent preliminary research findings conducted by the Gates Foundation in the Measures of Effective Teaching research study (2010). "Students' perceptions of a given teacher's strengths and weaknesses are consistent across the different groups of students they teach. Moreover, students seem to know effective teaching when they experience it" (MET Project 2010, 9–10).

CURRENT PRACTICES THAT CONTRIBUTE
TO COLLECTIVE EFFICACY

There are many professional researchers discussing the vehicles for creating and sustaining collective efficacy. Rick Dufour and Robert Eaker (1998) have coined the construct of Professional Learning Communities (PLC). The major characteristics of a PLC define the adult collaborative processes to improve achievement. The researchers at McRel (Marzano, Waters, and McNulty 2005) have enhanced these ideas by adding collective efficacy to their concept of a purposeful community.

In their construct, staff must have (a) agreed-upon processes, where all staff members provide input; (b) leverage their tangible and intangible assets; and (c) determine and accomplish a purpose that matters to all. In neither of these communities has the involvement of the learner overtly been described as a participant in the process or as an asset.

Douglas Fisher and Nancy Frey (2008) have described a process where if students need a learning concept, the teacher models a lesson ("I do"), then engages the learner in guided practice with the teacher ("We do"), then allows the students to learn together ("You do together") before releasing them for independent practice ("You do alone"). This provides for a collective efficacy between the teacher and the learner.

In areas such as technology the role of teacher may be in the younger person's hands and the role of learner is the adult. Patrick Higgins, a participant in a Fisher and Frey workshop during an Association for Supervision and Curriculum Development (ASCD) conference blogged that Frey said, "teachers know stuff; students know stuff; teachers and students learn from one another by interacting and collaborating." (Personal communication, March 14, 2009.)

Redefining collective efficacy to include and focus on the learners, the authors have explicitly coined the term, "learner-centric collective efficacy." In this construct, all the people in the school are learners *and* teachers and the purpose for collaborating is to enhance everyone's learning. The learners must be partners in the collaborative process within the school. In self-efficacy, there is a belief that the individual is capable; in collective efficacy, the teachers' belief is that the faculty together is stronger than each member is individually.

In learner-centric collective efficacy, which involves students in their learning process and the decisions of the school, the learner's individual efficacy and his or her contribution to the collective efficacy of the school is validated. When all stakeholders collectively contribute to a learner-centric efficacious school, the larger purpose of *proficiency for all* in the twenty-first century is within reach.

Creating a PDCA for Learner-Centric Collective Efficacy

The bad news is collective efficacy doesn't exist in many schools (DuFour and Eaker 1998, 2004). The good news is collective efficacy can be developed (Goddard, Hoy, and Hoy 2004), and it can be developed in learners as well. In creating a PDCA, staff and learners can continuously assess their progress using Hoy's (2009) Collective Efficacy Scale (CE-SCALE) to mark progress as one of their KPIs and determine the cycle times in which this assessment takes place.

Bandura (1997) proposed four sources of the development of collective efficacy beliefs: (a) mastery experience, (b) vicarious experience, (c) social persuasion, and (d) affective states. These sources have been researched with adults, and future studies need to include the learner to determine if these factors will generalize. The authors assert that it will.

Assessment on a collective efficacy scale. Hoy (2009) has developed a CE-SCALE, which is a twenty-one-item scale that measures collective efficacy in a school. It can be used with a staff to gather baseline data for individual and collective efficacy as well as set goals for improvement. The scale moderately and positively correlates between personal teacher efficacy when aggregated at the school level and collective teacher efficacy (r = .54, p < .01).

The authors suggest using this tool with older learners to determine if their impressions correlate with the adults. Research would need to validate this supposition. This tool and the results of formative and summative assessments will assist staff and learners to connect their effort, persistence, and resilience with results to collective efficacy.

Mastery experience: We did it before we can do it again. "A mastery experience is the most powerful source of efficacy information" (Goddard, Hoy, and Hoy 2004, 5). The perception that a group has been successful in the past raises the efficacy beliefs that performance will be proficient in the future. These past successes must be credited to internal and controllable variables, such as ability or effort. Goddard ([2001], cited in Goddard, Hoy, and Hoy [2004], 5) researched past school achievement and found that a "significant predictor of differences in teacher's perception's of collective efficacy was stronger than aggregate measures of race and socio-economic factors."

Mastery experience explained more than two-thirds of the variance among schools in collective efficacy beliefs. This finding has been replicated in the recent preliminary MET Project results, which found that "the teachers who lead students to achievement gains in one year or in one class, tend to do so in other years and in other classes" (MET Project 2010, 9). The following sources may explain the other one-third of the variance.

Vicarious experience: If they can do it, we can do it. "Vicarious experience is one in which the skill in question is modeled by someone else. When a model with whom the observer identifies performs well, the efficacy beliefs of the observer are most likely enhanced" (Goddard, Hoy, and Hoy 2004, 5). This may be as equally effective in organizational learning as individual learning. Borrowing from other organizations is a form of vicarious experience which can be as effective as firsthand learning (Dutton and Freedman [1985], as cited in Goddard, Hoy, and Hoy [2004]).

Social persuasion: Peer pressure. Social persuasion may entail encourage-ment or specific performance feedback from a supervisor or a colleague, or it may involve discussions throughout the community about the ability of the teachers to influence learners. PLCs invoke the power of social persuasion. This moves teachers from their personal reflection of the results of their practice to the group reflection of the practice and social support to try new practices.

These kinds of discussions may counter occasional setbacks that might have instilled enough self-doubt to interrupt persistence. The potency of persuasion depends on the credibility, trustworthiness, and expertise of the persuader (Ban-dura [1986], as cited in Goddard, Hoy, and Hoy [2004]).

In schools where there is a high degree of collective efficacy, new teachers learn that extra effort and educational success are the norm. This creates a press throughout the organization that encourages all teachers to do what it takes to excel and discourages stakeholders from giving up when facing adversity.

Affective states: United we stand! The level of feeling tone, either of anxiety or excitement, adds to individuals' perceptions of self-capability or incompe-tence. Organizations with strong beliefs in group capability can tolerate pressure and crises and continue to function without debilitating results. Strong schools get stronger and rise to the challenge when confronted; less efficacious schools are more likely to react dysfunctionally when confronted with a stressful condi-tion and this increases the likelihood of failure.

The principal must be the champion for the staff being a "cohesive group that can make substantive change" (Marzano, Waters, and McNulty 2005, 101). The authors would concur that depending on the magnitude of change, these efforts need to include the principalship, not just the principal. The principal-ship must use the leadership strategies of optimizer and affirmation (Marzano, Waters, and McNulty 2005).

"Optimizers inspire and lead new and challenging innovations. . . . Affir-mation recognizes and celebrates accomplishments and acknowledges failures." (Marzano, Waters, and McNulty 2003). Jonathan Supovitz and Jolley Bruce Christman ([2003], as cited and quoted in Brinson and Steiner [2007]), found that schools that achieved better results had leaders who provided opportunities for intense, ongoing instructional conversations using protocols that analyzed the correlation between teaching and learning. The role of leadership will be further discussed in section 4, *The Learner Improvement Cycle.*

Table 6.1. Creating the Culture of Learner-Centric Collective Efficacy Continua

Category	Beginning School	Developing School	Proficient School	Advanced School Meets All proficient Criteria, Plus
Preparing stakeholders for learner-centric collective efficacy	• Doesn't see that working together builds improved capacity in organization.	• Determines root causes for a lack of efficacy. • Looks for leverage points to improve collective efficacy. • Reinforces when collective efficacy is beginning.	• Assesses the collective efficacy culture of the school. • Uses an appropriate environment to build learner-centric collective efficacy and inducts new staff and learners.	• Creates opportunities for staff and learners, which embody learner-centric collective efficacy, to share with others. • Sees significance in work and is intrinsically motivated.
Goal-setting	• Settles for minimal expectations.	• Begins to set goals or more realistic goals based on data collected.	• Sets challenging goals based on data from the collective efficacy scale.	• Seeks challenging goals by digging into data (problem seeking).
Developing and hiring a knowledge and skill set	• Doesn't build learner-centric collective efficacy. • Accepts that outside influences overwhelm the efforts. • Doesn't use school's moral purpose or collective efficacy belief system in learning or professional development	• Assesses skills and knowledge of stakeholders on collective efficacy to determine individual and school-wide needs. • Develops and deploys knowledge and skill set in: Collective efficacy with a focus on the learner Norms for working together Internal and external locus of control Collaborative inquiry with data Understands teacher-learner partnership structure	• Trains new staff and learners annually in learner-centric collective efficacy. • Confronts new initiative or when "hits the wall"; evokes skill set to create learner-centric collective efficacy. • Checks for accurate deployment of knowledge and skill set based on identifying KPIs.	• Creates a moral compass that does not distract school's learner-centric collective efficacy from moral purpose (proficiency for all).

PLAN

PLAN	Recruiting staff	• Doesn't address learner-centric collective efficacy in recruiting or hiring process.	• Hires for an openness to new ideas.	• Creates a plan to hire for a reflective practice. • Recruits staff with skill set for creating a collaborative culture.	• Creates sustainability through recruiting and professional development to ensure continuation of collective efficacy.
DO	Creating learner-centric collective efficacy to improve achievement	• Doesn't see power of working together. • Doesn't build capacity in learners and staff to feel responsible for all learners. • Doesn't monitor learner-centric collective efficacy process and its connection to achievement.	• Begins to understand importance of teacher-student collaboration and sees success. • Directs students and staff to assist one another when help is needed. • Begins to apply learner-centric collective efficacy process.	• Believes that working together is more powerful than separate. • Builds capacity in learners and staff to independently help one another because they realize learner-centric collective efficacy enhances learning. • Uses skill set of learner-centric collective efficacy.	• Institutionalizes teacher-learner collaboration process into school culture and sustains it. • Develops processes in school where learners and staff take responsibility to teach each other when one is struggling. • Is seen as model of learner-centric collective efficacy process, supported by trends.
	Locus of control	• Attributes reasons for poor performance to external locus of control.	• Begins to develop an internal locus of control and holds self accountable for learning.	• Stakeholders take responsibility for results.	• Uses learner-centric collective efficacy strategies with new initiatives to build sustainability for all learners reaching proficiency.
	Persistence	• Puts forth minimal effort; sabotages positive efforts of others. • Gives up easily in the face of resistance or difficulty.	• Sustains short-term effort to solve less-complex tasks. • Is able to manage stress on short-term tasks.	• Demonstrates stronger efforts. • Persists in efforts to overcome difficulties to succeed.	• Puts forth strong effort and develops endurance in confronting challenging goals. • Increases morale through positive efforts.

(continued)

Table 6.1. *(continued)*

	Category	Beginning School	Developing School	Proficient School	Advanced School Meets *All proficient Criteria, Plus*
CHECK	Analyzing KPIs on cycle times	• Defends status quo. • Creates no measurement of collective efficacy.	• Evaluates KPIs of learner-centric collective efficacy on an *annual* cycle.	• Evaluates KPIs of learner-centric collective efficacy on a cycle or predetermined times.	• Evaluates KPIs of learner-centric collective efficacy on an accelerated basis.
ADJUST	Refining based on checking process	• Doesn't adjust practice based on KPIs.	• Begins to evaluate practices based on KPIs.	• Adjusts practices based on results of KPIs.	• Adjusts practices aligned with data collection on frequent cycle times.
	Improving continuously	• Doesn't see need to create processes for continuous improvement of learner-centric collective efficacy.	• Begins to examine current practices of continuous improvement and reinforces practices where learner-centric collective efficacy occurs.	• Validates and reinforces processes that allow continuous improvement of learner-centric collective efficacy to occur.	• Supports multiple cycles of continuous improvement to increase quality and results of stakeholder's working together.
	Celebrating	• Doesn't celebrate learner-centric collective efficacy.	• Celebrates learner-centric collective efficacy within stakeholder groups.	• Celebrates learner-centric collective efficacy between stakeholder groups.	• Posts data and celebrates with stakeholders when learner-centric collective efficacy has resulted in *proficiency for all.*

Suggested evidences:

➤ PDCA plans with KPI's and cycle times
➤ Anecdotal comments of internal locus of control
➤ Climate survey results about persistence
➤ Collective efficacy assessment used as baseline data and monitoring tool
➤ Collaboratively-created norms
➤ Share SMART goals based on collective efficacy

➤ Documents PLC agendas and growth data
➤ Hiring process/questions that include themes of collective efficacy
➤ Protocol for collaborative inquiry
➤ Documentation of celebration of collective efficacy
➤ Professional growth plans
➤ Data that collective efficacy has resulted in proficiency for all
➤ Learners and staff teaching each other in class and school-wide

LEARNER-CENTRIC COLLECTIVE EFFICACY: CONVERSATIONS WITH THE STAKEHOLDERS

Voices of the Principals

Question: "How do you link practice to develop collective efficacy in your school?" Chris Benisch uses social persuasion, affective states, and empowerment to build collective efficacy in his vertical teacher teams. He backward plans from what they need to have a plan that is monitored monthly. He sets up the structure and then empowers his staff "to own the solution," using tools from RISC such as guiding questions and the affinity diagram.

Kelly Williams used vicarious and mastery experiences to help her staff develop collective efficacy. She took her staff to two schools that were close to our demographics. They chose these schools because they had reached the tipping point in improving performance. She also shared her own experiences as a teacher in District 50 and the positive results she obtained from students as a mastery experience so her staff knew her coaching was effective when it came to teaching our district's children.

Sarah Gould says that collective efficacy can be built in the students through empowerment. "NWEA hasn't meant much to students in the past. Now that students know their scores and set goals, the test means something. Kids take ownership of their assessment scores."

When asked, "How do you celebrate with staff and students when collective efficacy is evident?" the principals had several relevant suggestions. Chris Benisch puts celebration and recognition on the agenda at the beginning of every meeting. He waits for staff to recognize one another before reading his list. However, he has to recognize some staff on an individual basis. There was a culture at his school of people not wanting to be recognized. For the students, he puts exemplars of goal-setting and capacity matrices in the hall for kids.

Williams reports the staff has taken over the staff meetings. Staff members want to show what they are doing and are fighting for the spotlight. Bill Stuckey says he uses choice breakout groups in the morning. He organizes tables with certain topics such as: goal-setting, data-driven dialogue, and progress monitoring. Teachers, who know the topics ahead of time, can go to the table they want, and bring examples to share.

Voices of the Teachers

Question: "How do you professionally develop or link past practice to develop collective efficacy?" Janelle Stastny feels the vertical team structure has created collective efficacy in her staff. She would miss other meetings before she'd miss a vertical team meeting now. This is different this year because of her implementation of SBS that started with the two model classroom teachers working together. Then the rest of the team got the training and they all started working together. They all saw the value of working together and the importance of vertically aligning.

Greg Russo discussed collective efficacy like this: "Teachers are getting that we are moving forward. Try this out, not do all of it, get some stepping stones and get their feet wet. We try to tell them it's do-able. It will lead to a learner-centric standards-based classroom. This is great stuff; you can implement it in baby steps." Everybody is doing things they've never been able to do before. It all happens with the shared vision as a starting point; from there, they use the tools.

Voices of the Learners

Question: "How are students motivated to help one another to create collective efficacy to raise achievement for the group?" They all reported being able to go to a list to see who was proficient at that skill. They liked the idea that they could go to another student and ask them for help. Anna said she knows the process to "see who's proficient and ask them for help." Maria and Penny both said they knew how to "go to a student who knows."

Voices of the Parents

Question: "How do you support the change efforts of the school to enhance the staff feeling good about working together to increase proficiency for your student?" Jason Reynolds shared stories from his daughter about the improvement with the engagement with her peers, how she raves about her teachers, and lets teachers know how she's changed at home. Joseph Maldonado pointed out the change from the beginning of the school year to now to staff: "That's been good!"

Key Points in Chapter 6:

1. What is the difference between teacher efficacy and collective efficacy for a school staff?

   Teacher efficacy is the perception of competence in the classroom but does not mean that the teacher is effective. Collective efficacy is the shared perception of the faculty that their shared efforts will have positive effects on students. The authors would contend that the students' perceptions need to be included in the perceptions of collective efficacy.

2. Why did the authors coin the term "learner-centric collective efficacy"?

   Learner-centric collective efficacy is the perception that everyone is a teacher and a learner and the collaboration between the learners and teachers enhances everyone's learning. This is a process that leads to reaching the attainable goal of proficiency for all in the twenty-first century.

3. How do you build learner-centric collective efficacy within a school culture?

   Learner-centric collective efficacy can be developed if it is not present within a school environment. Bandura believes that through mastery experience, vicarious experience, social persuasion, and affective states, collective efficacy can be built, and the authors would add that it must include the learner.

Section 4

THE LEARNER
IMPROVEMENT CYCLE

Learning is a result of listening, which in turn leads to even better listening and attentiveness to the other person. In other words, to learn from the child, we must have empathy, and empathy grows as we learn.

—Alice Miller

Children have to be educated, but they have also to be left to educate themselves.

—Ernest Dimnet

Fundamental components of section 4:

- The Learner Improvement Cycle Chart
- Creating the Learner Improvement Model
- Teacher's Role in Creating Learner Improvement
- The Learner Improvement Cycle Process
- Principalship's Role in Creating a Process for Learner Improvement
- Evidence for Implementing
- Staff's Knowledge and Skill Set to Implement the Learner Improvement Cycle
- Principalship's Role in the Learner Improvement Cycle Continua
- Key Points in Section 4

Guiding Questions in Section 4:

1. How are learners' roles emphasized in each step of the Learner Improvement Cycle?
2. What is the change in the teacher's role in the Learner Improvement Cycle?
3. How does backward-planning from the standards support the Learner Improvement Cycle?
4. What do principals need to know themselves as they develop the skills and knowledge in the Learner Improvement Cycle in their staff?
5. What is the principalship's role in developing a PDCA for staff to implement the Learner Improvement Cycle?

In the previous four chapters (chapters 3–6), the authors have described the prerequisite quintessential procedures a staff must undertake before a substantive change can be sustainable. Now, the successful implementation of creating a common moral purpose, being ready for the change, having a trust-to-doubt process, and developing collective efficacy with staff and learners will successfully launch the Learner Improvement Cycle.

In the following four chapters (chapters 7–10), we refer to the real change that needs to occur. Involving learners in their education, preparing them for twenty-first-century challenges and ensuring their proficiency is the ideal. This means the components of the teaching-learning cycle have transformed into the Learner Improvement Cycle. The process of charting the course involves using the cycle for learner improvement and then adjusting on a daily basis.

The *beginning teacher or principalship* is establishing their knowledge, skill, and usage in the Learner Improvement Cycle.

The *developing teacher or principalship* is building on their skills and knowledge in the Learner Improvement Cycle. They are starting to inform instruction based on standards and results.

The *proficient teacher or principalship* has established a competent skill set and begins to involve learners' input into the elements of the Learner Improvement Cycle.

The *advanced teacher or principalship* is at the advanced level of the continuum and exhibits an essential-progressivist philosophy. The *advanced teacher or principalship* collaborates with other staff members and learners within the school on the Learner Improvement Cycle, and ensures systems are in place to sustain and refine processes based on data.

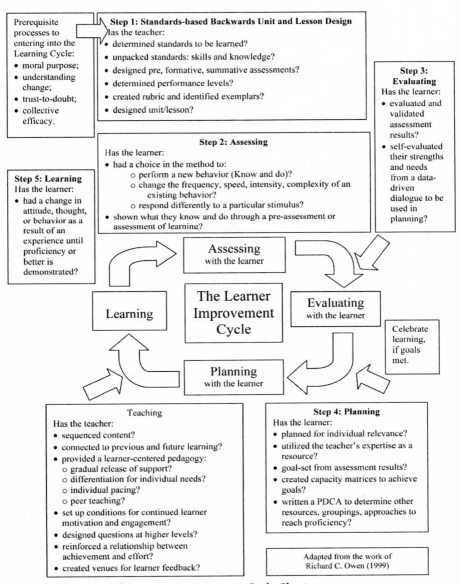

Prerequisite processes to entering into the Learning Cycle:
- moral purpose;
- understanding change;
- trust-to-doubt;
- collective efficacy.

Step 1: Standards-based Backwards Unit and Lesson Design
Has the teacher:
- determined standards to be learned?
- unpacked standards: skills and knowledge?
- designed pre, formative, summative assessments?
- determined performance levels?
- created rubric and identified exemplars?
- designed unit/lesson?

Step 3: Evaluating
Has the learner:
- evaluated and validated assessment results?
- self-evaluated their strengths and needs from a data-driven dialogue to be used in planning?

Step 2: Assessing
Has the learner:
- had a choice in the method to:
  o perform a new behavior (Know and do)?
  o change the frequency, speed, intensity, complexity of an existing behavior?
  o respond differently to a particular stimulus?
- shown what they know and do through a pre-assessment or assessment of learning?

Step 5: Learning
Has the learner:
- had a change in attitude, thought, or behavior as a result of an experience until proficiency or better is demonstrated?

Assessing
with the learner

The Learner Improvement Cycle

Learning

Evaluating
with the learner

Celebrate learning, if goals met.

Planning
with the learner

Teaching
Has the teacher:
- sequenced content?
- connected to previous and future learning?
- provided a learner-centered pedagogy:
  o gradual release of support?
  o differentiation for individual needs?
  o individual pacing?
  o peer teaching?
- set up conditions for continued learner motivation and engagement?
- designed questions at higher levels?
- reinforced a relationship between achievement and effort?
- created venues for learner feedback?

Step 4: Planning
Has the learner:
- planned for individual relevance?
- utilized the teacher's expertise as a resource?
- goal-set from assessment results?
- created capacity matrices to achieve goals?
- written a PDCA to determine other resources, groupings, approaches to reach proficiency?

Adapted from the work of
Richard C. Owen (1999)

Figure Section 4.1. The Learner Improvement Cycle Chart

CREATING THE LEARNER IMPROVEMENT MODEL

Based on work from the American Society for Quality website and the Teaching-Learning Cycle from Richard C. Owen, a model was developed for the components of good teaching and learning to be woven with a continuous improvement process. (See Figure Section 4.1) The foundations of both the quality and the teaching–learning model lie in assessing and evaluating results along the way, good planning, and quality tools. The purpose of our model is to illustrate a cycle that teachers, learners, and the principalship must utilize to create a system that will provide *proficiency for all.*

TEACHER'S ROLE IN CREATING LEARNER IMPROVEMENT

This model illustrates one complete Learner Improvement Cycle and the results may determine if the cycle needs to be repeated. For example, if the learner demonstrates proficiency during the assessment step, the learner could repeat the cycle for enrichment or begin a new concept. If a learner doesn't demonstrate proficiency during the assessment step, the teacher and learner will need to initiate another cycle until the learner reaches proficiency on the concept. If the learner is not making typical progress, the teacher will need to consult an interventionist and look for root causes.

Embedded in the model is a PDCA cycle to continuously improve and refine the process of each step. Teachers and learners begin each step *planning* together; this involves creating action plans with defined time lines, key performance indicators, and person(s) responsible with specific cycle times. During the *doing* phase of the cycle, the teacher and learner implement their plans and gather data. The *checking* phase causes the evaluation of that data on certain cycle times and *adjusting* occurs when needed. During the *adjusting* phase, it is important for teachers and learners to celebrate learning successes.

THE LEARNER IMPROVEMENT CYCLE PROCESS

Process prior to entering the Learner Improvement Cycle. The learning must be defined from a set of articulated and aligned priority standards (experts call them power standards, essential learnings [Reeves 2006; Ainsworth 2003]) or measurement topics (Marzano 2006). These priority standards will be determined through a district-wide process that identifies a guaranteed, viable curriculum (Marzano 2006) in each subject, in each grade level. This is a necessary precondition to enter the Learner Improvement Cycle.

Step 1: Standards-Based Unit and Lesson Design

Once the priority standards are determined, prior to entering the "Assessing" phase, components of backward, standards-based unit planning must be developed. Teachers must unpack the standards into the skills and knowledge that will be learned. This includes creating preassessments as well as formative and summative assessments, defining the performance criteria for proficiency, developing a rubric, and identifying exemplar samples. This all will support the development of the standards-based unit and lesson plans.

Step 2: Assessing

During step 2, the teacher will administer the assessment. On the first cycle, the learners will take the preassessment to determine where they enter the learning. During the unit, learners will focus on mastering specific learning objectives and engage in formative assessments. As learners and teachers agree that proficiency has been met through formative means, a summative assessment will be administered. The learner will approach the summative assessment with confidence due to demonstrating success on the prior formative assessments. This builds efficacy and a positive assessment culture.

Step 3: Evaluating

During the "Evaluating" step, the teacher must work with the learner to evaluate the quality of the assessment and the results of that assessment. Does the learner feel it is an accurate measure of his ability? Self-evaluating should occur prior to the learner turning in his performance assessment. The learner can self-evaluate his work prior to submittal, using a rubric or exemplar papers, which defines the performance levels.

If the results of the self-evaluation meet proficiency and the learner is confident in the quality of his learning, then a formal assessment should follow. If the results of this self-evaluation don't meet proficiency, the results lead to refinement of the learning. If the learner feels it is an accurate depiction of his skills and knowledge and understands his strengths and areas for growth, then the teacher and learner begin to plan the teaching episode to support the learning of new concepts.

Step 4: Planning

As the teacher and learner partner to begin "Planning" the learning, the learner's background, culture, interests, and experiences guide the relevance and differentiation of their learning. The learner and teacher begin their own PDCA process. They set goals and build a capacity matrix that will help the learner self-assess their progress on the skills and knowledge needed. In order to meet the individual needs of the learner, the teacher plans to adapt the materials, groups, instructional approaches, and learning environments.

Step 5: Learning

During the "Learning" phase, the teacher acts as a facilitator and now adapts the materials, groups, instructional approaches, and learning environment to partner with the learner. As the expert on content, the teacher activates prior knowledge and certifies that the information to be learned is valid and accurate. In a learner-centric classroom, the teacher uses his knowledge of the learner to motivate, make the learning relevant, and student-owned. The teacher is constantly asking questions, guiding the learning and the learner. This provides a feedback loop to improve the learning.

PRINCIPALSHIP'S ROLE IN CREATING A PROCESS FOR LEARNER IMPROVEMENT

There are continua in this section that describe the development of the principalship's beliefs and behaviors needed to create the culture for learner improvement for each of the four components, *Assessing, Evaluating, Planning, Learning*. Remember the principalship is not just the principal, but also includes assistant principals, instructional coaches, department chairs, team leaders, and many other teacher-leaders depending on the situation. In *School Leadership That Works*, Robert Marzano et al. (2005, pp. 108–9) state that a distributed leadership team must distribute twelve responsibilities focusing on the research-based effective school characteristics of:

(a) knowledge of the curriculum, instruction, and assessment;
(b) involvement in the curriculum, instruction, and assessment;
(c) intellectual stimulation;
(d) change agent;
(e) monitoring and evaluating;
(f) order;

(g) focus;

(h) flexibility;

(i) resources;

(j) discipline;

(k) outreach; and

(l) contingent rewards.

If a school is in second-order change, the principal may not be the only person who should lead this change initiative (Marzano et al. 2005). The principalship must act as "goodwill ambassadors for the second-order change initiative and act as liaisons between the faculty and administration" (Marzano et al. 2005, 121). The following describe the components of the principalship's continua.

Plan. The principalship is responsible for the creation of the overall plan, do, check, and adjust (PDCA) cycle of the processes that occur in the school. The PDCA is adapted from the construct of the American Society for Quality (www.asq.org/learn-about-quality/project-planning-tools/overview/pdca-cycle. html). It is the principalship's responsibility to create a plan with the staff and learners to identify KPIs and cycle times to monitor the results.

The principalship must then determine the effectiveness of the plan, maintain promising practices, and retire practices that are not yielding results. This cycle allows for planning for continuous improvement and sustainability. One way to sustain improvement is by recruiting staff members who have the skill and knowledge set in the Learner Improvement Cycle. Another component of the planning phase is aligning tools and processes in order to create a school that applies the Learner Improvement Cycle in a systemic and systematic manner.

Principals motivate their staff through creating a common moral purpose and shared vision. Instead of leading through rules and procedures, the principal must engage the staff's hopes and commitments (Dufour and Eaker 1998). James Kouzes and Barry Posner (2006, 111) depict this process as describing a compelling vision of our future together, appealing to others to share in that vision, and showing staff how their long-term interests will be realized by engaging in the shared vision.

Do. "Learning is what most adults will do for a living in the 21st century" (Perelman 2009). As a principal who leads from the middle (Dufour and Eaker 1998) instead of the top, the principal must be the lead learner (Kohm and Nance 2007). In Douglas Reeves' (2002, 130) Leadership for Learning Continua Matrix, two of his quadrants (Leading and Learning) show a "high understanding of the antecedents of results and that replication of success is likely." In both of these cases, the leader looks and digs deeply into the data and determines if the leader and staff have the needed knowledge to solve the problem.

The principal must engage in the cycle of *not knowing* (admit what she doesn't know) to *knowing* (learning) and back again (Kohm and Nance 2007).

This entails questioning her own mental models and building new ones. "If school staff wants students to develop a sense of responsibility for their own success, evaluate their own work, articulate what they've learned, and recognize the power they have over their own learning" (Kohm and Nance 2007, 154), the leader needs to model and risk becoming the lead learner. The chart (Table Section 4.1) and the adjoining continua (Table Section 4.2) outlines the unique knowledge and skill set needed to be learned and implemented by the principal and staff for each component of the Learner Improvement Cycle.

Capacity must be built for those who are taking on new roles (Fullan 2005). Staff can't learn this just from a workshop, but it must be undertaken in the daily implementation of the new skills learned from the workshops. Michael Fullan (2005, 72) believes stakeholders "can't trust well-intentioned people if they are not good at what they are doing." People in demanding cultures must confront incompetence and ascertain whether the staff members are capable of change or unwilling to change. "School cultures that are associated with improvement are far more demanding than other cultures" (Fullan 2005, 73).

To address the issues of school drop-out, low achievement, and achievement gaps, educators are calling for more learner-centered practices (APA 1997). It is imperative to involve the learners in every component of the Learner Improvement Cycle. By blending essentialist and progressivist philosophies, students are the hub of their education and become insistent learners. This blending takes into account the APA learner-centered practices and achieving proficiency on the content standards. "Learner learning, facilitated by teachers and over time directed by learners themselves, is individualized to learners' needs, and every strategy is used to ensure that learning is maximized" (Delorenzo et al. 2009, 78).

Check. Fullan (2005, 14) states, as one of his eight elements of sustainability, that having "intelligent accountability and vertical relationships" pulls together both capacity building and accountability for staff. Some call this notion providing "pressure and support" for staff. This is a contentious issue as the principalship must serve as both the evaluator and coach.

Change is hard. A component of the accountability process is whether the new practices are working or if they need improvement. Staff evaluation criteria should be emblematic of the behaviors of the common moral purpose. Conversations focused on improvement can be difficult without a shared vision. Fullan (2005) believes that there are certain non-negotiables (shared vision or common moral purpose) that hold stakeholders accountable. Hopefully these non-negotiables reduce the level of conflict, but if they don't, then there may be a misalignment of an individual's and the common moral purpose.

It is in this step where the staff analyzes KPIs on cycle times to ensure the plans are accomplishing the intended goals. If continuous improvement is the desired outcome, correlating the action plan components with the quantifiable KPIs will provide trend data to benchmark improvement over time.

Adjust. During the adjust phase, the staff must adjust practices that are not yielding results based on the KPI progress. This allows for the sustainability of successful efforts to be replicated and unsuccessful efforts to be retired. As a part of the sustainability plan, the staff needs to recognize opportunities for celebration in the design, refinement, and/or results of these processes. As a component of Thomas Sergiovanni's School Leadership Framework (2001), principals who display symbolic leadership model important goals, and establish rituals and celebrations that acknowledge what the school and community see as important. It is vital to include all stakeholder groups in these celebrations.

EVIDENCE FOR IMPLEMENTING

Under each teacher continua of the Learner Improvement Cycle is the beginning of a list of evidences that school staff should consider when developing themselves using these continua. These are meant to be a starting point for a school to begin to collect key performance indicators and artifacts that will allow them to benchmark their progress toward the proficient or advanced criteria.

After tables Sect 4.1 and 4.2 that describe the skill and knowledge set needed to be developed in the principal and the staff and the needed actions for principals to take, the authors begin the four chapters of the Learner Improvement Cycle. Each of the four components of the Learner Improvement Cycle (Assessing, Evaluating, Planning, and Learning) will be detailed in a chapter, which will contain the latest research through a learner-centric, standards-driven lens and then outline the actions needed for teachers and learners to successfully implement.

Table Sect 4.1. Staff's Knowledge and Skill Set to Implement the Learner Improvement Cycle

Standards-Based Unit and Lesson Design	Assessment Skill Set	Evaluating Skill Set	Planning Skill Set	Learning Skill Set
• Planning for standards-driven backward units • Unwrapping standards/assessment frameworks • Designing pre-, formative, and summative assessments • Writing a rubric • Choosing exemplars • Develop capacity matrices • Writing standards-based lesson plans • Choosing appropriate instructional strategy (approaches, groupings, resources)	• Collaborating on learner-centric assessments • Motivating learners through assessment practices • Using of taxonomy • Identifying Guaranteed Viable Curriculum-Learning targets/objectives • Designing of pre-, formative, and summative assessment based on a learning target • Assessing the reliability and validity of assessment • Scoring assessment with inter-rater reliability • Determining levels of learning (skill, analytical, contextual) • Aligning of performance levels on assessments • Choosing exemplars	• Evaluating assessment results through a data-driven dialogue • Unpacking the standards to tie to assessment questions • Self- and peer-evaluating • Utilizing cognitive coaching techniques • Practicing collaborative inquiry • Determining reliability and validity of assessments • Identifying error patterns	• Planning for learner-centric instruction • Understanding the power of and planning collaboration with colleagues and learners • Planning for gradual release of support • Implementing Lesson Study Models • Using assessment information (data) to inform instruction • Giving learner feedback • Creating a learner profile • Writing ILPs for learners • Writing SMART Goals • Progress monitoring through RtI • Differentiating for process, product, and content • Creating capacity matrices	• Peer-teaching • Utilizing direct instruction, content knowledge • Implementing research-based instructional strategies • Increasing learner engagement • Modeling for learners • Aligning teaching and mastery of standards • Questioning strategies • Developing learner-centric shared vision and code of conduct • Creating rubrics (teachers and learners) • Adjusting instruction based on learner's feedback • Increasing ownership of learning • Adapting to learning styles • Creating enrichment/reteaching activities • Connecting hands-on experiences to abstract concepts • Creating relevant learning experiences/interdisciplinary units • Celebrating learning

Table Sect 4.2. Principalship's Role in the Learner Improvement Cycle (LIC) Continua

	Category	Beginning Principalship	Developing Principalship	Proficient Principalship	Advanced Principalship Meets All Proficient Criteria Plus
PLAN	Planning	• Has no knowledge of practices • Doesn't plan for continuous improvement process.	• Determines root causes to interpret results • Looks for leverage points to improve results.	• Plans implementation of specific components of the LIC. • Creates KPIs, timelines, person responsible, actions.	• Formalizes plan and process to implement and plans for the documentation of multiple iterations to refine.
	Creating a culture to motivate change	• Doesn't understand how to motivate staff for change.	• Creates a culture where teachers change to be compliant or please the principal.	• Creates culture where teachers feel they cannot do a good job teaching without a quality LIC and without learner involvement.	• Inspires staff and learners to create, use, and monitor LIC.
	Developing a knowledge and skill plan	• Doesn't plan for development of an assessment knowledge or skill set.	• Assesses skills and knowledge of staff on assessments to determine individual and school-wide needs.	• Puts together a short-term professional development plan that individualizes for each staff member and group needs.	• Puts together a long-term professional development plan that individualizes for each staff member and group needs.
	Recruiting staff	• Doesn't address LIC in recruitment or hiring process	• Recruits staff with some of attributes of skill and knowledge set for LIC.	• Recruits staff with skill and knowledge set in LIC to improve learning.	• Creates sustainability through recruiting and on-going professional development for LIC.

(continued)

Table Sect 4.2. *(continued)*

	Category	Beginning Principalship	Developing Principalship	Proficient Principalship	Advanced Principalship Meets All Proficient Criteria Plus
DO	Implementing a teacher knowledge and skill set	• Doesn't implement the professional development plan for teachers.	• Implements specific skill sets in involving learners in Standards-based Unit and Lesson Design, Assessing, Evaluating, Planning, Learning for teachers (Table Sect 4.1)	• Monitors use of knowledge and skill set in school.	• Ensures a process where knowledge and skill set is renewed and sustained in the staff.
	Involving students	• Doesn't involve learners in LIC.	• Begins to provide venues for learners to give feedback in their involvement in the LIC.	• Ensures learners are involved in all aspects of Assessing, Evaluating, Planning and Learning.	• Ensures learner ownership of Learner Improvement process. • Ensures learners design method and content of how they will show what they know and can do.
	Analyzing KPI's on cycle times	• Defends status quo. • Has no cycle time to evaluate data.	• Evaluates KPIs on an <u>annual</u> cycle.	• Monitors KPI process and product on a cycle or predetermined times.	• Analyzes KPIs on accelerated cycles.

CHECK	Evaluating staff	• Doesn't hold staff accountable for criteria on staff evaluation tool. • Doesn't connect teacher performance to learner performance.	• Gives staff specific feedback using the evaluation tool, but doesn't follow-through to hold staff accountable. • Begins to connect teacher performance to develop a professional development plan for individuals or groups.	• Holds staff accountable on the evaluation tool for appropriate use of knowledge and skill set in the LIC. • Correlates teacher placement on the evaluation tool to learning.	• Solicits feedback from staff and learners to refine evaluation tool. • Replicates best teacher practices based on improved learning. (status and growth data).
ADJUST	Refining based on checking process	• Doesn't adjust practices.	• Begins to make adjustments based on anecdotal data.	• Adjusts based on results of gathering quantitative and qualitative data on KPIs at cycle times.	• Adjusts practices in line with data collection on more frequent cycle times. • Use learner-led process to adjust practices based on feedback.
	Celebrating successes	• Doesn't celebrate successes with staff.	• Begins to see benefit of celebrating successes with staff.	• Celebrates with staff and learners.	• Celebrates alignment of systemic and systematic practices.

Key Points in Section 4:

1. How are learners' roles emphasized in each step of the Learner Improvement Cycle?

   The learner becomes an integral partner in each step of the Learner Improvement Cycle. The end results must answer the question: "Do the steps of the cycle improve student learning?" The learners need to have an opportunity to choose their appropriate method of assessment, evaluate the results of that assessment, plan for relevancy and setting goals, and access resources that will result in learning. This happens within a collaborative classroom environment where the learners are constantly giving and receiving feedback for improvement.

2. What is the change in the teacher's role in the Learner Improvement Cycle?

   The teacher's role becomes more of a facilitator of the learning environment and a collaborator with the learner to improve their learning. The teacher still provides direct instruction when the learner needs it.

3. How does backward-planning from the standards support the Learner Improvement Cycle?

   The teachers must identify the priority standards, unpack the standards and create the pre-, formative, and summative assessments before planning the resources, groupings, and approaches to support each learner.

4. What do principals need to know themselves as they develop the skills and knowledge in the Learner Improvement Cycle in their staff?

   Principals need to understand they must be as knowledgeable as their staff. They must self-assess their level of skills and knowledge and cultivate themselves as instructional leaders in the areas of developing standards-based unit and lesson design; assessing, evaluating, planning; and teaching and learning.

5. What is the principalship's role in developing a PDCA for staff to implement the Learner Improvement Cycle?

   The principalship must create a PDCA cycle that involves having a plan, recruiting the right staff, creating the tools and processes they will need, professionally developing the staff, involving the learner, ensuring accountability and celebrating results.

· 7 ·

Assessing: Assessment in the Learner Improvement Cycle

Fundamental components in chapter 7:

- Teachers' and Learners' Role in Assessing
- Teachers Know Their Content
- Developing Rubrics
- Design of Preassessments and Formative Assessments
- Matching Assessment Practices to the Type of Learning
- Learner Involvement in Assessment
- Teacher's Role in Assessing in the Learner Improvement Cycle Continua
- Assessing: Conversations with Stakeholders
- Key Points in Chapter 7

Guiding Questions in Chapter 7:

1. How does a staff establish a collaborative assessment culture?
2. What are the differences between assessment "for," "of," and "as" learning?
3. What is the learner's role in assessing?

TEACHERS' AND LEARNERS' ROLES IN ASSESSING

Creating Assessment Culture

The culture in which educators design, deliver, and utilize assessments set the stage for the learner-centric environment. If assessments are designed with the young people, the learners perceive assessments as tools to ascertain the areas for their improvement, and learners will look forward to assessments as a natural part of their learning (Stiggins 2008). However, if assessment content and processes are kept a secret from the learner and the results used to rank and sort students, assessments will be perceived as an entity outside of the learning process and something to be feared (Stiggins 2008).

Creating a culture to refine assessments and assessment practices is vital for the leadership of the school. W. James Popham (2008) defines four levels of formative assessment. The first three levels consist of the uses of formative assessment data and will be discussed in *The Planning* chapter.

The last level consists of a school-wide adoption of formative assessment practices through the use of professional development and learning communities. Popham describes two strategies, professional development and use of Teaching Learning Communities (TLCs), which should be used by the staff of a school to be effective; principals must take the lead in designing the conditions for these two strategies to occur.

> Professional development concerning assessments should include: (a) definitional clarity regarding the nature of formative assessment, (b) reliance on assessment-elicited evidence to help teachers and learners make improvement-focused adjustment decisions, and (c) honest appraisals of the degree to which particular procedural variations in the formative assessment are supported by research and reason.
> The use of TLCs is where groups of teachers work together over an extended period of time to strengthen their individual curricular, instructional, or assessment skills. (Popham 2008, 109–20)

Uses of collaborative inquiry for teachers and learners. Richard DuFour and Robert Eaker (1998) use a process in PLCs for teachers to work together in collaborative inquiry to improve their work. Nancy Love and associates (Love et al. 2008) assume that collaborative inquiry is a necessary process for teachers to focus on teaching and learning and make effective use of data in order to improve results for learners. "They develop ownership of the problems that surface, seek out research and information on best practices and adopt or invent and implement the solutions they generate" (Love et al. 2008, 6).

This collaborative inquiry process can also be used for students to engage in their learning. Mary Hamm (Hamm and Adams 2002, 3) cites that in a collaborative classroom "teachers provide time for students to grapple with problems, try out strategies, discuss, experiment, explore, and evaluate."

Uses of assessment. In *Classroom assessment and grading that work*, Robert Marzano (2006, 3) outlines four generalizations about the use of formative assessments:

> Feedback from classroom assessments should give learners a clear picture of their progress on learning goals and how they might improve,
> Feedback on classroom assessments should encourage learners to improve,
> Classroom assessment should be formative in nature, and
> Formative classroom assessments should be frequent.

Both Marzano and Rick Stiggins agree that learners should have access to frequent specific feedback on their performance which should motivate them to improve their performance.

Stiggins, in his *Assessment Manifesto* (2008, 1), passionately calls for the "reevaluation, redefinition, and redesign of assessments' role in the development of effective schools. The work, to be done, is so crucial as to require urgent pedagogical, social, and political action." He believes there are two purposes for creating balanced assessment systems: (a) productive instructional decision making and (b) productive assessment dynamics and learner success.

Assessment Informs Instruction, Identifies Standards, and Provides for Program Evaluation

There are three main uses for assessment: (a) to inform the next steps in instruction, (b) to determine which standards are being mastered, and (c) to make program evaluation decisions. To inform instruction, teachers need to gather "continuous evidence of each student's current location on the scaffolding leading to each standard" (Stiggins 2008, 4). To determine which standards are being mastered, teacher leaders and principals must collect "periodic, but frequent, evidence" (Stiggins 2008, 5) across classrooms. This step emphasizes the PLC work being done by teams in many schools today.

Finally, to determine which programs are contributing to raising achievement, superintendents and school boards must collect the data from yearly assessments that will reveal how many learners have mastered the essential standards, based on participation in that program. This will move the educational communities' thinking beyond the two former purposes of assessment *"for"* learning and *"of"* learning (Stiggins 2008).

Assessment to Encourage Learning

To create productive assessment dynamics that lead to learner success, assessments must be looked at from the learners' point of view (Stiggins 2008). For too many years, assessments were used to rank students along a continuum. Little or no thought was given to the effect the assessment results had on the learner. How learners felt about their assessment results was compounded by class ranking and resulted in a continuum of able and non-able learners.

Able learners saw themselves as capable learners, confident in school, which gave them the emotional strength to take risks for more success. Non-able learners failed to master the early prerequisites within the allotted time, so then failed to learn what followed. This early failure resulted in a loss of confidence and "deprived them of the emotional reserves to continue risk-trying. Students own interpretation of assessment results influenced their confidence and willingness to strive on" (Stiggins 2008, 7).

Definition of Formative Assessment–Assessment for Learning

Assessment must be the first component in any Learner Improvement Cycle. It is imperative to know what learners know and are able to do before proceeding in the cycle. The most effective and timely way to determine this is the use of formative classroom assessments. Popham's (2008, 6) definition for classroom formative assessment (which is a derivative of a definition from SCASS [State Collaborative on Assessment and Student Standards 2006]) will be used: "Formative assessment is a planned process in which assessment-elicited evidence of students' status is used by teachers to adjust their ongoing instructional procedures or by students to adjust their current learning tactics."

Stiggins et al. (2007, 41–42) pose three questions that support students assessing for learning accompanied with strategies to answer each question:

1. Where am I going?
   Strategies: (a) Provide a clear and understandable vision of the learning target,
   (b) Use samples and models of strong and weak work.
2. Where am I now?
   Strategies: (a) Offer regular descriptive feedback,
   (b) Teach learners to self-assess and set goals.
3. How do I close the gap?
   Strategies: (a) Design lessons to focus on one aspect of quality at a time,
   (b) Teach learners focused revision,
   (c) Engage learners in self-reflection, and let them keep track of and share their learning.

Many times this is an overlooked step in the cycle as teachers jump into teaching without the learners knowing their strengths and needs through assessment.

Assessment as Learning

A third type of assessment has emerged in the literature. "Assessment AS learning is any practice which takes the 'what to improve' into 'how to improve'" (Clarke 2008, 9). Shirley Clarke differentiates *Assessment FOR Learning* as the vehicle for identifying the concept to be improved and *Assessment AS Learning* as what takes it to the instructional step of how it will be improved. She combines these two descriptions into her definition of formative assessment.

Definition of summative assessment–assessment of learning. Both formative and summative assessments have their place in education for very different purposes. Stiggins' (2004, 33) definition for summative assessment (assessment *of* learning) will be used: the practice that (a) "documents individual or group achievement or mastery of standards"; (b) "measures achievement status at a point in time for purposes of reporting"; and (c) "accountability."

Stiggins adapted the work of Chappius and Chappius (2002) to define the typical uses for this type of assessment and the role of stakeholders in using the results. Typical uses are: (a) determining learner competence, (b) sorting learners according to their performance, (c) promotion and graduation decisions, and (d) grading.

Learner's role in summative assessment is to (a) study to meet the standards, (b) take the test and try to achieve the highest point value possible, and (c) avoid failure. The teacher's role is to (a) build and administer the test in a valid testing setting, (b) use the test results to help learners achieve the standards, (c) assist parents in understanding the assessment results, and (d) interpret and report the results on the grade card.

TEACHERS KNOW THEIR CONTENT

Creating a Guaranteed, Viable Curriculum (GVC)

Teachers must have access to a guaranteed, viable curriculum prior to creating assessments. Community input is vital to define the concepts that are important not only to live in the community, but now in a global society. The skill and knowledge set needed to prepare graduates for postsecondary and workplace environments are virtually the same (American Diploma Project 2004).

Learners must have a firm foundation in literacy and numeracy skills but also the "twenty-first-century soft skills" of creativity, problem solving, collaboration, adaptability, initiative, persistence, and responsibility (Partnership for the 21st Century 2008). Currently, assessment strategies of these twenty-first-century skills are few and far between.

In order for a curriculum to be guaranteed, essential content must be taught and learned. All students must have learned the set of skills that is considered essential for all learners. Learners may then have access to what is considered supplemental, if there is time (Marzano 2003).

The viability of the curriculum is that it must be able to be taught in the available time allotted (Marzano 2003). Currently, there are too many standards identified and too little time to teach each one to mastery. This tension has caused some teachers to try to teach all the standards, but the outcome is that they can only teach them superficially or they "pick and choose" their favorite standards and teach those in-depth. This creates a nonguaranteed, nonviable curriculum.

Even if teachers have a guaranteed, viable curriculum, this does not assure learners that they have a teacher with the background knowledge of the GVC. Our learners will not be proficient if our teachers do not have mastery of their content.

Developing a Learning Progression

Teachers must define a learning progression in order to build effective classroom formative assessments. "A learning progression is a sequenced set of sub-skills and bodies of enabling knowledge that students must master in order to master a more remote curricular aim" (Popham 2008, 24). Ainsworth (2003) calls this process "unpacking the standards." These progressions provide guidance to teachers of what to assess and when to assess. Popham (2008, 35–41) describes a four-step process to accomplish this:

Understand the target curricular aim thoroughly,
Identify all requisite precursory sub-skills and bodies of enabling knowledge,
Determine whether learners' status, with respect to each preliminarily identified building block, can be measured, and
Arrange blocks in an instructionally defensible sequence.

Teachers must design assessment queries that will align to these sub-skills in order for learners and teachers to know where learners need to enter the learning sequence.

DEVELOPING RUBRICS

After creating a learning progression, it is vital for learners, teachers, and parents to understand and agree on the criteria needed for learners to be successful. Most rubrics (or scoring guides) are designed to delineate between unsatisfactory, partially proficient, proficient, and advanced work on the measured essential learnings (Popham 2008). These essential learnings can be derived from the criteria in the learning progression.

Marzano (2006) states that rubrics should be given to students to be written in student-friendly language prior to the commencement of new learning and used to evaluate and give learners specific feedback on the progression of their learning. In a learner-centric environment, rubrics should be written *with* the learners and they should self- and peer-assess their work along with teacher feedback.

Defining Proficiency

Marzano has spent years developing a universal rubric structure (2006, 41). It defines the performance standard (proficient) as score "3" items that comprise the simple and complex information and skills that were taught to the learner. Score "2" (partially proficient) identifies the basic details and simple information that is relatively easy. If the score "2" and "3" concepts and skills can be accomplished only with help, it indicates a score "1" (unsatisfactory). Score "4" (advanced) is evidence of knowledge and skills that goes in-depth and beyond what was taught in class. Learners should have input in the design of projects or assessment alternatives that would show their proficiency level.

Defining a Public Standard

In 1995, Linda Darling Hammond and associates raised the issue of assessing students against an academic and public standard (Darling-Hammond, Ancess, and Falk 1995). In most schools, students are assessed against an academic standard with little or no connection to the public standards in which they will be judged upon once leaving the academic world. So many times learners ask the question "When will I use this?" and teachers, some who have little experience outside of a K–12 academia setting, cannot provide examples. Teachers need to understand the relevancy of their content in the real world so they can teach and assess their learners with that relevancy of a public standard in mind.

Public standards are the standards that learners must meet when entering the job market, college, or the military. Colorado is currently defining the criteria for workplace and postsecondary readiness (Colorado Department Education Postsecondary and Workplace Readiness, www.cde.state.co.us, June 30, 2009). Academic standards need to be better aligned to these public standards. In an effective assessment program, learners must be able to communicate to an authentic audience what they now know and are able to do and be evaluated by that audience on a public standard.

To this end, teachers must deliver the relevant content through thematic units where learners must synthesize multiple content learning in real-world settings (Delorenzo et al. 2009). This also provides teachers and learners with relevant experiences so *they* can connect the content in meaningful ways. This step must be a precursor to the development of authentic learning experiences and assessment against a public standard.

DESIGN OF PREASSESSMENTS
AND FORMATIVE ASSESSMENTS

In order to acculturate useful assessment practices in a school, a staff must design and administer appropriate formative classroom assessments. This includes preassessment as well as classroom formative assessment practices. The interpretation of those assessments will be left to *Evaluating* in chapter 8. The staff must create, monitor, and evaluate the preassessment and formative assessment process and learners' results to assure its validity and reliability.

Staff must be trained on reliable testing practices in order to maximize learners' ability to show what they know and can do through an assessment process. Staff must be aware of barriers that can occur and affect learner results. Within the assessment context, staff must mitigate "(a) noise distractions, (b) poor lighting, (c) discomfort, (d) lack of rapport with the assessor, (e) cultural insensitivity in the assessor or the assessment, and (f) lack of proper equipment" (Stiggins et al. 2007, 115). These context factors should also be assessed by the learner.

This will give the learner and teacher another data point to evaluate the results of the assessment. By constructing useful pre- and formative assessments, the school staff is setting in motion the critical first step in the Learner Improvement Cycle.

MATCHING ASSESSMENT PRACTICES
TO THE TYPE OF LEARNING

In the creation of assessments, whether they are formative or summative, the type of assessment must match the type of learning required. Learners should be able to demonstrate thinking at all levels of a taxonomy (Bloom's, Marzano's), and assessments should draw that type of thinking from the learner.

The following paragraphs outline the teaching and assessment strategies that teachers and learners must design together in order to align the level of learning expected from students with the appropriate assessment strategy (a) knowledge and comprehension in the classroom; (b) application, analysis, synthesis, and evaluation in the classroom; and (c) synthesis and evaluation of skills and knowledge in a real-world setting.

When knowledge and comprehension learning is expected, direct teaching should be the mode of instruction. In assessing at the knowledge and comprehension level, the assessment should be accomplished by forced-choice items, which include: "(a) multiple choice, (b) matching,

(c) alternative choice, (d) true/false, (e) fill-in-the-blank, and (f) multiple response" (Marzano 2006, 77–78).

When asking students to apply higher-level thinking in their learning in the classroom, the teaching should be accomplished through modeling and the gradual release of support (I do, we do, you do together, you do) (Fisher and Frey 2008). The assessments would then be accomplished through small group/individual projects; demonstrations; oral responses and reports; and/or open-ended problems (Delorenzo et al. 2009).

In assessing higher-level thinking and learning in a contextual setting (using analysis, synthesis, evaluation in context), teaching in the field is required. The assessment practice should consist of constructing an authentic problem, learning from a master in the field, and assessing against a public standard (Delorenzo et al. 2009; Darling-Hammond, Ancess, and Falk 1995).

LEARNER INVOLVEMENT IN ASSESSMENT

Contributing to Assessing Knowledge and Skills

Learners can contribute to the assessment process in a number of ways. They can contribute questions for the teacher's consideration, or for an assessment that they believe will best show what they know and can do. Learners can suggest assessment methods that they design to meet the standards. They can practice the expected skills and knowledge, self-assess their skill level, and alert the teacher when they are ready to be assessed on the expected learning.

This is in contrast with current practice where all students are tested on the same day, in the same way. By placing this ownership of assessment in the student's hands, learners are motivated to show their teachers what they know and can do. This has been evidenced by District 50's students anxiously waiting for an appointment with their teacher to be assessed.

Creating Capacity Matrices

Learners can play an integral role in the assessment process. They can help to create a capacity matrix that will delineate the skills needed to master a standard. In the District 50 model, learners are invited to help unpack the standards and create a capacity matrix with the learning progression defined. Learners will then self-evaluate their progress. (This will be explained more in chapter 8, *Evaluating*.)

In Figure 7.1, secondary learners are asked to unpack the standards, create a PDCA cycle for their learning, reflect on their learning, and self-assess their progress on their learning in a capacity matrix.

Student Goal-setting and PDCA	Name:					
Learning Target(s) addressed: Content: Personal/Social:						
SMART Goal:						
Date Started:		Anticipated Finish Date:				
Relevancy: Why am I learning this? How does it apply to my long-range goals?						
Plan: What do I already know and can do? How will I know I'm on track (KPIs and cycle times)?						
Do: What will I do to achieve my goal and by when?						
Check: How will I check my progress? What evidence will I show to meet my goal?						
Adjust: What adjustments can I make if I'm not on-track to meet my goal? How does my level of effort match my achievement?						
Reflection: How did my PDCA work? What woul I do differently next time?						

Capacity Matrix	1	2	3	4	Type of Evidence	Effort Score- Self Assess on a 1-4 scale
	I can demonstrate what I've learned with help	I learned the simple parts	I learned the simple and complex parts	I apply learning in creative and unique ways		
Simple Skills			XXXXXX	XXXXXX		
Simple Knowledge			XXXXXX	XXXXXX		
Learning Target				XXXXXX		
Score 4 Demonstration						

Figure 7.1. Example of a PDCA and Capacity Matrix

Table 7.1. Teachers' Role in Assessing the Learner Improvement Cycle Continua

	Category	Beginning Teacher	Developing Teacher	Proficient Teacher	Advanced Teacher Meets All Criteria of Proficient, Plus
PLAN	Identifying KPIs and cycle times for assessing	• Doesn't identify KPIs for effective assessing. • Doesn't identify KPIs for assessing with learners.	• Begins to identify KPIs for assessing but does not align actions and time lines to achieve. • Begins to create process to assess with learners.	• Identifies KPIs, actions, and cycle times of an effective assessment culture and processes. • Identifies KPIs, actions, and cycle times for assessing with learners.	• Involves learners in the process of identifying KPIs, actions, and cycle times regarding learner involvement in effective assessing.
	Has deep knowledge of content standards	• Doesn't have complete content knowledge in teaching area.	• Has some content knowledge but doesn't have depth of understanding to explain concept for struggling learners.	• Utilizes deep knowledge of content/standards to make knowledge relevant to learners.	• Has deep knowledge of content and plans for interdisciplinary connections. • Mentors others in content. • Creates new knowledge-action research in classroom.
	Identifying a guaranteed viable curriculum	• Doesn't plan for all learners mastering guaranteed, viable curriculum (GVC).	• Begins to identify GVC that all learners must know and master.	• Plans for learners reaching proficiency on GVC.	• Plan to go beyond GVC to assure proficiency on skills and knowledge that apply GVC in a new and/or creative manner.

(continued)

Table 7.1. *(continued)*

	Category	Beginning Teacher	Developing Teacher	Proficient Teacher	Advanced Teacher *Meets All Criteria of Proficient, Plus*
PLAN	Aligning assessment and standards	• Doesn't align standards to assessment items so learners are unclear.	• Creates assessment and then assigns standards to assessment.	• Determines what learners need to know and be able to do from standards, then creates assessment. • Communicates to learner how assessment is aligned to standards.	• Creates a capacity matrix by standard with learners to chart their progress.
	Matching type of knowledge to assessment	• Doesn't create and align assessments with type of skill, analytical, or contextual knowledge on which a learner must be proficient.	• Builds assessments that accurately measure skills but struggles with authentic assessments for analytical or contextual knowledge.	• Assures appropriate assessment matches type of skill, analytical, or contextual knowledge in which learners must show proficiency.	• Supports learners in their design of assessments of demonstrated skill, analytical, or contextual knowledge in unique ways.
	Creating criteria of performance levels	• Doesn't define performance levels of proficiency for learner.	• Begins to define criteria for all levels of proficiency, but criteria are vague and do not support learner understanding.	• Creates specific criteria for all levels of proficiency and builds rubric/capacity matrix. • Gathers exemplars to model proficient work.	• Collaborates with learners to create specific criteria for rubrics/capacity matrices. • Learners gather exemplars to post for other learners' use.
	Creating a preassessment for new units	• Doesn't preassess learners' skills and knowledge.	• Gives preassessments that only assess low-level thinking (knowledge/comprehension).	• Creates preassessments (knowledge → analysis) that inform learner and teacher what learner knows and is able to do to be used in evaluating results/planning.	• Creates preassessments collaboratively with learners in similar courses using all levels of a taxonomy (knowledge to evaluation) based on standards.

DO	Creating assessment options	• Doesn't give learner choice or involvement.	• Gives learners limited choices of how to demonstrate skill and knowledge.	• Provides learners with assessment options to show proficient or advanced performance on standards and gives learners choices, when practicable.	• Collaborates with learners to choose or write appropriate assessment for type of skill and knowledge to be demonstrated (skill, analytical, contextual).
	Self- and peer-assessing	• Doesn't use a rubric for assessment and learners don't know learning expectation.	• Uses a teacher-created rubric to assess learners' work but does not involve learners in process.	• Involves learners in translating teacher rubric criteria to kid-friendly language to assess proficiency on an academic standard.	• Collaborates with learners to self- or peer-assess work with use of a learner-created rubric to enhance self-directed learning against an academic and/or public standard.
	Administering assessment within a reliable context	• Doesn't know potential barriers in the assessment context.	• Begins to be aware and attempts to mitigate the barriers that can occur in an assessing context.	• Mitigates the barriers that can occur in an assessing context.	• Elicits feedback from learners on the effect of assessing context barriers on the learner's performance.

(continued)

Table 7.1. (continued)

CHECK	Checking the assessing process	• Doesn't check KPI's on a regular cycle.	• Checks KPI's infrequently and doesn't monitor for refinement.	• Checks the assessing process based on the KPI's so that adjustments can be made.	• Has learners evaluate the effectiveness of the assessing process by checking KPI's.
	Checking for reliability and validity	• Uses classroom assessments that are not reliable and/or valid.	• Relies heavily on text as resource for designing assessments, not a learning progression of standards. • Begins to develop formative classroom assessments that benchmark learning of standards throughout a unit.	• Develops assessment that is reliable and valid; accurately measures standards through a learning progression. • Develops classroom assessments of standards that are based on learning targets, with learners.	• Works with learners and colleagues to define a learning progression and design classroom assessments that correlate with performance on high stakes assessments based on standards.
	Using collaborative inquiry	• Doesn't use collaborative inquiry process to create and refine assessments.	• Begins to collaborate with other teachers to create and refine assessments.	• Writes assessments with colleagues that align definition of proficiency for classroom assessments, grading, and high stakes testing environments.	• Writes common formative assessments with colleagues and learners to gather a profile of learner work to measure proficiency levels. • Adjusts assessment based on collegial conversation.
ADJUST	Adjusting teacher /learner assessment process	• Doesn't adjust assessment practices.	• Makes ineffective adjustments assessments that won't affect the KPI's.	• Adjusts assessments based on checking KPI's in a timely manner.	• Has learners adjust assessments based on feedback from teachers / peers during checking.

ADJUST				
Using assessments to inspire	Doesn't write assessments with building learner confidence and efficacy in mind.	Writes assessments that begin to build efficacy to assist learners in identifying strengths. Identifies non-strengths as challenges, not weaknesses.	Inspires optimism, persistence, and efficacy in learners through construction of appropriate assessments.	Collaborates with learners to sustain assessments that continue to build optimism and persistence.
Identifying exemplar papers	Doesn't show learners exemplar papers of what it means to be proficient.	Uses exemplars to define proficiency in a teacher-driven process.	Uses definition of proficient to choose learner work as exemplars based on rubric. Teaches learners to self-assess work with exemplars and refine until work is proficient or advanced.	Encourages learners to advocate updating exemplars that better exemplify criteria on rubric.

Suggested evidences:
- PDCA plans to build an assessment culture, with KPI's and cycle times
- Improved student learning and performance moving towards *proficiency for all* as measured by multiple indicators, both formative and summative
- Evidence of deep content knowledge on transcripts, licensure tests and in practice in classrooms
- Evidence of the use of a GVC in unit and lesson plans
- Teacher-designed formative assessments: pre-assessments, benchmark assessments, classroom assessments that are aligned to standards and types of learning required
- Evidence of learners' involvement in creating their own assessments, rubrics, and capacity matrices for self- and peer-assessing
- Identified common definition and learner exemplars of proficiency) criteria
- Feedback on assessment concerning the assessment context.
- Learners' use of capacity matrix to measure proficiency on standards, based on assessments
- Articulated common formative assessments based on a taxonomy
- Climate survey results that indicate teacher's self-motivation to create pre-assessments and formative assessments.
- Professional development documentation for knowledge and skill set for assessment
- Pre-assessments and common formative standards-driven assessments posted in a common place for all staff to use (e.g. intranet website, hard copies kept in dept)
- Calendars for cycles for summative and formative learner assessments
- Evidence in daily practice that formative assessments are being used to inform instruction: Align learning progressionàformative assessmentàlearning targetà teaching and learning activity
- Learner reflection sheet that evidences assessment is a helpful tool and not discouraging their learning

ASSESSING: CONVERSATIONS WITH THE STAKEHOLDERS

Voices of the Principals

Question: "How do you create culture for preassessments and involvement of students in their assessments?" Bill Stuckey discussed how using preassessment builds a foundation for differentiating instruction. "When teachers give a preassessment, kids who have previous knowledge of that topic don't need to waste time on that topic, they can go on . . . which leads into data-driven dialogue so you can have the dialogue with the kid and know their strengths and weaknesses and know where they need to work in a learner-centered classroom."

Chris Benisch added that the teachers compared their preassessments and their results in third through fifth grade in vertical teams, ensuring inter-rater reliability between teachers, so kids can use this information to set goals.

Voices of the Teachers

Question: "How does assessment create hope for students and their learning?" They all used preassessments to provide the data for students to determine their learning goals. No longer is assessment only a summative event where students have to guess what's on the test and never get to continue learning the skills and knowledge they missed.

Jennifer Rizzo describes this as "a more hopeful system; before they got an 'F,' filed it away, now, they have to analyze *what* they need to fix, *why* they didn't pass, and re-do it." Rizzo celebrates with students when they've achieved their learning targets by placing their name on a "Wall of Fame" (class experts). This is used for all learners to learn from one another, which creates a cooperative attitude.

Janelle Stastny told a story about "Joey," who continually struggled with his learning and got a 50 percent on a preassessment. By the end of the unit, he was so proud because he had earned a 90 percent and told Stastny that "I finally like learning." Stastny sent home a note praising "Joey" and his mom came in to talk with her in disbelief and asked, "Are you sure he got a 90 percent on an assessment?" "Joey" is now being used in the class as a peer teacher.

Greg Russo told this anecdote: "I've spent so much time to get it (formative and summative assessments) totally aligned. When they're (the students) showing up and they think they're ready to take the summative assessments, they show me their formative assessments and they are all proficient, we already know they're going to be proficient on the summative. If they show me their formative assessments and they've been *emerging, emerging,* and they come up to me, and say I'm ready to take the posttest, I say, 'Well, you can take the posttest, but what do you think you're going to get on these (emerging) parts?' The student says 'Not well.' What's a better use of your time taking the posttest or working on these areas?' Then they are confident when they take the postassessments."

The teacher's role has changed in a learner-centered classroom. Stastny has created a flowchart with her students to guide their problem-solving during their independent work time on formative assessments. The flowchart described options to be used when the teacher is busy with a group: ask a peer, go to their book, skip the problem, or raise their hand and finally ask the teacher. As Stastny was checking in with the kids' groups to see if they needed help, the student pointed to her flowchart and said, "See, Mrs. Stastny, we're not to you, yet!" Teachers truly become the facilitators of very independent learners.

Anne Marie Dadley described the results of using rubrics and assessments at parent–teacher conferences. She had several bright kids who were scoring the proficient or "B" level. Parents at conferences fussed with their students saying, "You know what to do to get an A, now get busy and do it."

Voices of the Learners

Question: "How do you know what it takes to be successful on each assessment?" Anna described a process in her class where the teacher puts the proficiency on the board, and the "students who are proficient on that skill can help the ones who are not." She says they take a pretest to see "where we're at and what we know. Whatever we don't know, then we study on it and then we take a posttest and see if we get proficient."

Students reported feeling differently about assessments in their new system. Maria told of different kinds of tests. She stated that now when she knows about the test and knows what's going to be on the test then she's "not scared." Penny agreed that tests now "help you learn more, you learn the bad subject and if you don't know the problem, then you study it." Anna reports that her teacher goes over the information to be tested. When she's studying, she hears her teacher's voice, "Are you sure that's the right answer? I hear her voice in my head."

Voices of the Parents

Question: "Do you know your child's level of proficiency on standards and how do you know?" Jason Reynolds responded that his daughter is excited and looks forward to the challenge of taking a test. Now that she can "re-do," it has changed her opinion of what tests are about. Tomasita Perri said, "Teachers are getting more involved now, not trying to use tests to punish the students. The teachers make the students make up the work to get the students to where they need to be, get them caught up."

Joseph Maldonado said the teachers showed him charts and graphs to indicate where his child was. Reynolds describes that the teacher shared his child's scores with him. The teacher explained what his child needs to be able to do at grade level, showed the strengths and areas for growth, and shared the kind of questions they asked, so he could help her.

Key Points in Chapter 7:

1. How does a staff establish a collaborative assessment culture?
   Current PLC structures need to expand to involve learners in the assessment process. Teachers need to develop formative assessments with colleagues to improve the assessments. Teachers need to provide frequent feedback to learners on their assessments so they know what they have accomplished and look forward to learning what they don't know yet. Formative assessments should encourage learning, not rank and sort learners.

2. What are the differences between assessment "of," "for," and "as" learning?
   Assessments serve many different purposes. "Assessments of learning" are summative assessments that provide information for accountability. "Assessments for learning" inform instruction based on an event. "Assessments as learning" are embedded in the learning activities; learners can't distinguish the assessment from the learning.

3. What is the learner's role in assessing?
   The learner's role is to determine the most appropriate method for pre-, formative, and summative assessments. The learner is preassessed to determine where his skills and knowledge compare to the standards at the beginning of the learning. The learner collaborates with the teacher in creating rubrics to monitor her progress on formative (for learning and as learning) assessments. The learner also is involved in providing exemplars of proficient work. The learner needs to provide maximum effort on formative and summative assessments so teachers can depend on the accuracy of the results.

Evaluating: Evaluating in the Learner Improvement Cycle

Fundamental components in chapter 8:

- Teachers' and Learners' Role in Evaluating
- Evaluating Assessment Results for Learning
- Evaluating the Assessment
- Evaluates for Use in Planning Instruction
- Teacher's Role in Evaluating in the Learner Improvement Cycle Continua
- Evaluating: Conversations with Stakeholders
- Key Points in Chapter 8

Guiding Questions in Chapter 8:

1. How have teachers' and learners' roles shifted in evaluating the results of the assessments?
2. What do students use to evaluate their learning prior to submittal?
3. How is learning evaluated so learners receive authentic feedback?

TEACHERS' AND LEARNERS' ROLES IN EVALUATING

Teachers' and learners' roles must change in a learner-centered environment. Current assessment practices are no longer sufficient. If "participation, equality, inclusiveness, and social justice" (Hargraves and Fullan [1998], as cited in Rolheiser and Ross [1998, 3]) are valued, then the teacher must begin to share leadership and responsibility for evaluating assessments with students to improve their learning.

This extends democratic principles (Rolheiser and Ross 1998) to the learners and parents to share in the assessment practices. There are two purposes for this involvement: (a) to refine the learning for the learner and (b) to hone the assessment instrument and process to better align to standards and communicate its intended purpose.

EVALUATING ASSESSMENT RESULTS FOR LEARNING

Stiggins et al. (2007, 153) uses the assessment for learning three-question process (Where am I going? Where am I now? How can I close the gap?), and the focus of evaluating assessment results is on the second question, "Where am I now?" In order to answer this question, teachers must offer learners regular and specific feedback and teach learners to self-assess for goal-setting. It is of critical importance that the instructional decisions are made by learners *and* teachers, working in collaboration (Stiggins 2008).

Teacher and Learners Collaborating in a Data-Driven Dialogue

Learner-centric assessment fosters collaboration and depends on increased learner-faculty contact (Huba and Freed 2000, 24). During this collaborative time, the teacher and learners engage in the four steps of a data-driven dialogue (adapted from Wellman and Lipton [2004], by the Colorado Consortium for Data-Driven Dialogue [2004]).

The teacher and learners *predict* what they believe the results of the assessments will be and expose their own biases.

The teacher and learners *explore* the results of the assessments and write factual statements about the results. At this time, the teacher and learners do not attempt to provide reasons why the results are as they are.

The teacher and learners begin to take the factual statements and *explain* why the results have occurred.

The teacher and learners utilize those explanations to set goals and *take action* for new learning, relearning, or adaptations.

These are used in the next step of the Learner Improvement Cycle for planning and goal-setting.

Validate Accuracy of Results against Standards

As learners become a consumer of assessment information, they develop a strong sense of control over their academic well-being. Learners truly become partners with their teacher (Stiggins 2008, 10). Rick Stiggins believes it is important that a learner is able to show what she knows and can do accurately on an assessment because there will always be an emotional reaction to results, which determines what the learner does next. If there are low results and the learner tried hard and cared about the results, this leads to failure to take risks and hopelessness. If there are high results and the learner worked hard to succeed, he will feel efficacious and will keep trying; hope and sustained effort is maximized.

So the question becomes, how do we keep learners "believing that success is within reach if they keep trying"? (Stiggins 2008). By giving learners the criteria on which they will be assessed and the skills to self-assess prior to submittal, learners will learn the information at their own pace to proficiency because the learning target is clear.

Use of Rubrics and Exemplars for Academic and Public Standards

The use of rubrics and exemplars gives all learners the criteria for proficiency prior to the beginning of the work. The learners know the skills and knowledge they will need to produce for a piece of evidence to document proficiency or better. Their self-evaluation of the quality of their work against the rubric and/ or exemplars prior to submittal involves the learner actively in this step of the learner improvement process. In a learner-centered environment, "all students know the standards for excellence and therefore have a chance to produce excellent work" (Huba and Freed 2000, 47).

The instructor is not the only, or even perhaps the most important, evaluator. All engaged in the learning process have a stake in serving as assessors. Having public standards creates an environment that is fundamentally fair, downplaying the current need to figure out the system. "As the student population becomes increasingly more diverse, public standards of excellence ensure fairness for all" (Huba and Freed 2000, 47).

Learner Self-Evaluation Process

Best practice requires that the learner be actively involved in the creation of the rubric criteria. Learners must also be involved in utilizing the rubric to self-evaluate. Self-evaluation is defined as "students judging the quality of their work, based on evidence and explicit criteria for the purpose of doing better work in the future" (Rolheiser and Ross 1998, 1).

There is an explicit four-stage model for teaching learner self-evaluation skills that involves learners in: "(a) defining the criteria, (b) applying the criteria, (c) receiving feedback on their self-evaluation, and (d) developing productive goals from that information" (Rolheiser and Ross 1998, 4–5). Current practice of many teachers often omits the third stage of this process, which provides a venue for teachers to help learners hone their self-evaluation skills.

When learners begin to self-evaluate, they evaluate themselves imperfectly and need feedback (from teacher and peers) on their attempts to implement the criteria. This self-assessment provides learners with the information about their own improvement and their current status, when they need it (Stiggins 2008).

EVALUATING THE ASSESSMENT

Stiggins et al. (2007, 107) suggests five steps in the development of assessments: (a) plan for the intended use of the assessment and identify the learning targets and the method to assess them, (b) develop the test items and scoring guides, (c) critique it prior to administering the assessments, (d) administer the assessment, and (e) revise the quality of the assessment, based on the results, as needed. The focus of this section is on the last component of this process: revise the quality of the assessment, based on results.

Participating in Collaborative Inquiry Process to Refine Assessments

Learners need to be a component in the refinement of the assessment process. In *Professional Learning Communities* (DuFour et al. 1998), teachers come together, evaluate a collaboratively designed assessment, analyze the results, and refine the assessment. Better yet would be to involve the learner in a dialogue with the teacher to see (a) if the assessment was understood by the learner and (b) gave learners the opportunity to show what they knew and were able to do.

The teacher and learner would engage in a cognitive interview where the learner would do a think aloud about what the question is asking and how the learner would answer the question (Willis 1999).The teacher can then take this data and pilot refined assessment questions, collaboratively designed with the learner.

Validate Accuracy of Results

During this collaborative dialogue, the teacher and learner determine if the assessment accurately assesses the standards that it intends, and matches the learner's understanding. Guiding questions (Stiggins 2008, 115) should be:

Is the assessment a credible source of the learner's academic success?
Was the assessment structured so the learner could show his or her best
   learning?
Were there barriers within the learner that distorted the results?
Were there barriers within the assessment environment?
Were there barriers within the assessment itself?
Was there bias in the questions for certain learner groups?

"For assessments to yield dependable results, they must meet standards of quality. These standards of quality include assessment that: (a) are designed to serve a specific predetermined purpose, (b) arise from a specific definition of achievement success, (c) are designed to specifically fit into each particular purpose and target context, and (d) communicate their results effectively" (Stiggins et al. [2006], as cited in Stiggins [2008, 6]). Assessments of high quality are sensitive enough to detect and accurately reflect changes in learner achievement that evolve over time.

If "classroom, interim benchmark, and state assessments are not accurate enough or sensitive enough to detect changes, the assessment will not contribute to productive assessment systems or school improvement" (Popham [2008], as cited in Stiggins [2008]). Once points of refinement have been identified, the teacher is obligated to adapt the portion of the assessment that violates the standards of quality.

EVALUATES FOR USE IN PLANNING INSTRUCTION

"The opportunity to self-correct and try again is essential to self-improvement and the development of lifelong learning skills; this is the underlying premise of continuous improvement" (Huba and Freed 2000, 47). In the next chapter, learners and teachers will now take the results of this evaluation step and begin the process of setting goals for new learning, relearning, or continued learning.

Table 8.1. Teachers' Role in Evaluating in the Learner Improvement Cycle Continua

Category	Beginning Teacher	Developing Teacher	Proficient Teacher	Advanced Teacher Meets All Criteria of Proficient, Plus
Identifying KPIs and cycle times for evaluating	• Doesn't identify KPIs for effective evaluating. • Doesn't identify KPIs for evaluating with learners using their assessment results.	• Begins to identify KPIs for evaluating but does not align actions and time lines to achieve. • Begins to create process to evaluate with learners.	• Identifies KPIs, actions, and cycle times of an effective evaluating process. • Identifies KPIs, actions, and cycle times for evaluating with learners about their assessment results.	• Involves learners in the process of identifying KPIs, actions, and cycle times of evaluating the quality and validity of assessments. • Involves learners in the process of identifying KPIs, actions, and cycle times of effective evaluating their assessment results.
Planning for evaluating assessment results	• Doesn't have a plan for evaluating the accuracy of assessment results to inform instruction or involve learner.	• Begins to plan for teacher evaluation of assessment results.	• Creates a plan to involve learners in evaluation of their assessment results.	• Involves learners in planning process for evaluating assessment results.
Planning to evaluate the quality of the assessment/ assessing process	• Doesn't have a plan for evaluating the accuracy of assessment tool or process.	• Begins to plan for teacher evaluation of assessment tool or process.	• Creates a plan to involve learners in evaluation of the assessment tool or process.	• Involves learners in planning process for evaluating assessment tool or process.

PLAN

DO	Evaluating assessment of the standards	• Is unaware of correlation of assessment items to standards.	• Is aware that assessment items must be aligned to learning targets based on standards.	• Examines assessment with learners to check for alignment of skills and knowledge and their level of learning.	• Correlates results of common formative assessments to results of summative assessments. • Uses data to predict performance on future summative assessments.
	Creating rubrics for academic and public standards	• Doesn't provide evaluative expectations at beginning of an assignment.	• Lists elements needed in an assignment but provides no qualitative descriptors for each element.	• Creates rubric criteria for self-evaluation with learners.	• Teaches learners how to create the criteria to develop their own rubrics.
	Self-evaluating work on rubrics and exemplars	• Doesn't provide opportunities for learners to self-evaluate.	• Provides learners a rubric prior at the beginning of an assignment.	• Provides opportunity for learners to compare and contrast own work against a rubric.	• Expects learners to use *their* critical thinking skills to self-evaluate work prior to submittal, based on criteria on a rubric. • Provides opportunity for learners to compare and contrast own work against an exemplar paper.
	Using a data-driven dialogue	• Provides grades to learners on a work sample.	• Provides descriptive evaluative feedback to learners on a work sample.	• Engages learners in a data-driven dialogue: predict, explore, explain, and take action.	• Facilitates the independent utilization of the data-driven dialogue process by learners.

(continued)

Table 8.1. *(continued)*

	Category	Beginning Teacher	Developing Teacher	Proficient Teacher	Advanced Teacher Meets All Criteria of Proficient, Plus
DO	Refining assessment and validating accuracy of results	• Doesn't elicit feedback from learner.	• Analyzes items on assessment, evaluates if items tested were effectively taught.	• Facilitates discussion with learners as to whether assessment gave learner a chance to demonstrate their best work.	• Involves learners in item analysis of test and elicits feedback from learners on quality of test item and effective teaching/learning.
CHECK	Checking evaluating process	• Doesn't seek input from stakeholders on evaluating process.	• Solicits input only from teachers on evaluating process.	• Solicits feedback from learners on evaluating process on KPIs.	• Empowers learners to review evaluating process based on KPIs.
ADJUST	Adjusting the evaluating assessment process based on results	• Doesn't refine the evaluating assessment process based on feedback.	• Begins to adjust the evaluating assessment process based on feedback received.	• Incorporates feedback into a refinement of evaluating assessment process based on the results.	• Integrates learners into creation of new evaluating assessment process.

Suggested evidences:

⋗ PDCA plan with KPI's and cycle times.
⋗ Improved learner performance toward proficient and advanced.
⋗ Class lists/groups regrouping based on evaluating results.
⋗ Data is collected and report generated by disaggregated subgroups.
⋗ Learners articulate their results on assessments.
⋗ Learner reflection sheet on the 4 components of a data-driven dialogue.
⋗ Reflection sheet for learners to evaluate their draft or final results of their work based on a rubric or exemplar paper.
⋗ Reflection sheet that supports learners' self-evaluation on a public standard rubric.
⋗ Feedback form that shows learner input on improving assessments.
⋗ Feedback form that shows learner input on ways to improve learner results.
⋗ Feedback sheet that shows teachers' specific feedback to learner on their self-evaluation.
⋗ Schedules of staff's collaborative time to evaluate assessment data
⋗ Follow-through that ensures accountability through minutes or principal's attendance at meetings focused on an inquiry protocol
⋗ Professional growth plan based on evaluating assessments and results of assessments
⋗ Reflective question template (concerning evaluating assessment results) completed with staff's reflection.
⋗ Report that shows correlation of common formative assessment and summative assessment results.

EVALUATING: CONVERSATIONS WITH THE STAKEHOLDERS

Voices of the Principals

Question: "How have you used feedback from students to evaluate and improve the assessment program at the school?" They reported that it's about involving students and giving students choice. Bill Stuckey reported that his teacher, Greg Russo, has created a system where students design their assessments from their preassessment results. Sarah Gould said the primary teachers at her school are experimenting with a format that they think works best for their students *by asking the students*. Chris Benisch reported his teachers are asking the kids to help design the centers from the results of their preassessments.

Voices of the Teachers

Question: "How do you involve students in evaluating error patterns to inform instruction?" All the teachers working in learner-centered, standards-driven environments reported having more time and specific rubrics to work with students to identify their error patterns. The ability to provide immediate teacher feedback is a true asset. Anne Marie Dadley explained that "I know my students so much more because I have so much time to work with them individually. I give feedback on writing immediately against the six traits. I can show them their errors right away and they can see their own error patterns that match what I'm saying." Robin Kietzmann developed her own rubric to help pinpoint where the students were making their mistakes.

Greg Russo explains his system, where students self-assess and elicit peer-assessment before the teacher and student assesses and evaluates the results. "For each assessment, I have them do, for the formative assessments along the way, I throw a blank rubric on the top. Before I ever grade it, they have to self-assess, and get a peer-assessment, and then (he or she) gives it to the teacher." He continues, "When they submit the formative assessments, I grade it right there."

Students must be taught how to provide constructive feedback to their peers. Both Jennifer Rizzo and Janelle Stastny describe processes in their classroom that involve peer-assessment of student work. Rizzo calls it "Glow and Grow" where the classroom community grades work together on a rubric. The students see all levels of work and what advanced exemplars look like. Students are very honest with their peers. Stastny has students peer-assess their journals and has taught them how to give constructive feedback.

Dadley uses a data-driven dialogue to help middle-school students evaluate their results. Students *predict* where they think they will be on the assessment, *explore* the results, *explain* what the results mean, and then set goals for *taking action*.

Jess Rapp, Dadley's teammate, describes her process for her students' evaluation of assessment results. The day after students take an assessment, they complete an "error analysis" for that assessment. Error analysis is a data-driven dialogue process, where students predict their proficiency, record their overall observations of their assessment, and then analyze each question for any errors. During the analysis, students must demonstrate (with help from peers or a teacher, if necessary) that they know the correct process for completing a problem. Students complete the error analysis/data-driven dialogue process even if they are proficient overall.

Teachers were asked, "How do you collaborate with other teachers to evaluate the results of assessments, refine the assessments, and appraise the instruction you conducted?" In Adams County School District 50, teachers collaborate in several different structures. Some teachers meet in vertical teams and others work with same-grade level content partners. Each group works on their Monthly Action Plans (MAPs) in order to increase the inter-rater reliability between teachers. Some of the barriers to this process are that teachers have differing philosophies. Kietzmann reports this process begins to make these philosophical stances more obvious.

Dadley agrees that in her school "everybody was at such a drastically different point in the change process and had such strong ideas; there was a high degree of frustration. Some wanted to hear what others had to say, some thought they were already doing it, some never were." Stastny concurs that sometimes teachers are not willing to listen and accept help from one another because their egos are in the way.

Russo explains that the current PLC model of the monthly MAP meetings has to change in a learner-centered environment. In the past, teachers all gave the same assessments and brought the results for content partners to examine and refine their inter-rater reliability. Now students "are working on different assessments at different paces, so I might only have eight out of twenty-five papers to look at. Now we have to compare against examples of proficiency and hone the exemplars of proficient. The student and I decide (if the work) is proficient, then discuss that with a colleague and see if there is agreement on what is proficient."

Voices of the Learners

Question: "How do you know your work is proficient before you even hand it in?" Anna said, "Ms. Rizzo has a rubric that has grammar and spelling on it and then we'd get graded on it. It has helped us to know what proficient is." Penny described how she graded herself, and could see (regarding the skills and knowledge) "where you're advanced at, graph it, if you go down, then you have to study more about that. If you're proficient, then you get to go to the next thing."

Voices of the Parents

Question: "How are you a partner with your child's teacher in understanding the results of the assessments?" Jason Reynolds said it would be essential to "make sure the parents understand how important the assessments are. If a child understands how important it is to you, then he will pay more attention." Tomasita Perri added that parents can assist in the "motivation to want to be higher."

Key Points in Chapter 8:

1. How have teacher's and learner's roles shifted in evaluating the results of assessments?
   Teachers and learners collaboratively engage in a data-driven dialogue to determine the validity of results and begin the planning process for instruction. Learners give the teacher feedback as to whether the assessment was accurate in measuring their skills and knowledge, and give feedback on the validity of the questions on the assessments.

2. What do learners use to evaluate their learning prior to submittal?
   Learners use rubrics to self-assess their work based on prescribed criteria. Learners also contribute exemplars of work that exemplify the range of proficient work. They then compare their work against these rubrics and exemplars. The opportunity to self-correct must be provided to learners so they can self-improve.

3. How is learning evaluated so learners receive authentic feedback?
   Learners need the opportunity to present their assessment projects in front of an authentic audience and receive feedback using a public standard.

Planning: Planning in the Learner Improvement Cycle

Fundamental components of chapter 9:

- Teachers' and Learners' Role in Planning for Instruction
- Backward-Planning Using the Learner Progression
- Informing Instruction
- Learner-Centric Preplanning
- Teacher's Role in Planning in the Learner Improvement Cycle Continua
- Planning: Conversations with Stakeholders
- Key Points in Chapter 9

Guiding Questions in Chapter 9:

1. How are learners involved in planning, which has traditionally been a teacher-driven activity?
2. How do we plan for the individual needs of learners through SMARTER goals?

TEACHERS' AND LEARNERS' ROLES
IN PLANNING FOR INSTRUCTION

Planning may be the most important and least utilized step in the Learner Improvement Cycle. It takes a growth mentality to properly plan for the needs of each learner (Clarke 2008). Teachers with a growth mindset versus a fixed mindset realize that learner intelligence can be increased. Shirley Clarke asserts that learners can use planning to be the vehicle of their own intelligence enhancement. Teachers must realize that collaborative planning with learners can be a major influence on the learning of the students in their class.

Teachers and learners, together, (a) must reveal the learners' background and development in order to embed relevancy into their planning, (b) need to understand the learning target and the learning progression of subskills and enabling knowledge in order to backward-plan for their proficiency, (c) must use the results of assessments to plan and set goals, and (d) plan the occasion and triggers for instructional and learning tactic adjustments (Popham 2008).

CONSIDERING LEARNER BACKGROUND
AND DEVELOPMENT TO BUILD RELEVANCY

Creating Learner Profiles

The American Psychological Association (1997) outlines a set of fourteen learner-centric principles to "provide a framework that can contribute to current educational reform and school redesign efforts." The *Developmental and Social Factors* and *Individual Differences Factors* both guide the creation of a learner profile. The teacher and learner must collaboratively create the learner profile, which should include the unique developmental characteristics of each learner to include: (a) physical, (b) intellectual, (c) emotional, and (d) social factors.

The profile should also include the traits of each learner's background to include: (a) language, (b) ethnicity, (c) race, (d) beliefs, (e) socioeconomic status, and (f) experience. By collecting this information on every learner, the teacher can reference this information in planning for learning to build relevance for the learner. Learners now know more about the major influences on their learning.

Standards-Driven Unit Planning

Based on the original work by the Centennial BOCES (1997), through a Goals 2000 grant, the state of Colorado entered the standards movement after the state passed legislation to create the Colorado Model Content Standards in 1993. This backward-unit-planning work must be revisited in light of involving learners in this planning and brought to fruition to truly hold learners accountable for reaching proficiency on the standards.

Teachers must create a learning progression of standards to be accomplished and backward-plan the content to be learned. W. James Popham (2008, 24) defines a learning progression as the "sub-set of sub-skills and bodies of enabling knowledge that it is believed that students must master enroute to mastering a more remote curricular aim." Robert Marzano (2006) defines this subset in his rubric of skills as "score 2's" or "basic" that scaffold to the curricular aim of his "score 3's" or "proficient."

BACKWARD-PLANNING USING THE LEARNING PROGRESSION

Initially, in a standards-driven classroom teachers must determine what standards must be mastered, arrange them into a learning progression, cluster them together in a unit of study, write pre-, formative, and summative assessments and then determine the success criteria for learners to reach proficiency. The teacher will then determine the array of instructional strategies that would best suit the content and the learners.

The teacher and learner will determine how to differentiate those strategies based on the needs of the learner. Then the teacher chooses the possible resources and approaches to accomplish the attainment of the standards. This unit plan is then delineated into learning targets/objectives for daily lesson plans.

Writing Learning Targets/Objectives from a Learning Progression

As the teacher discusses the learning with the student, ensuring the learning target is written with the appropriate level of rigor is vital. The learner must also understand the success criteria needed to show proficiency (Clarke 2008, 80).

Learning targets/objectives, written for teacher use, must be translated with the learner into student-friendly language to ensure this understanding. Learning targets/objectives should be written with the audience, content, skill, performance, assessment criteria understood by all. Prerequisite skills and knowledge may need to be incorporated to scaffold students to this learning target/objective as well. Learners can then build their capacity matrices based on these skills and plan for the new learning.

Using Assessment Results and Qualitative Learner Feedback

The teacher and learners must use the evaluation of assessments to confirm the plans for each learner in order to move this planning process to be learner-centric. Based on the individual results of the assessment, each learner will enter the learning progression at different points along the continuum of skills and knowledge. Teachers and learners will identify the learning targets to be learned and organize them into SMARTER goals and an Individualized Learning Plan (ILP) in order to put the teaching and learning into motion.

INFORMING INSTRUCTION

Writing SMARTER Goals with Learners

Learners must be involved in writing their own SMARTER goals. Remember that a SMART goal must be specific, measureable, attainable, results-driven, and time-bound (DuFour and Eaker 1998).

In teaching learners the SMARTER goal process, learners must learn how to write a goal in this manner with an easier content, something more familiar before transferring that knowledge to the new content to be learned. From this SMART goal, action plans for future actions must be created to achieve this goal. To add to the continuous improvement cycle of a SMART goal, the "ER" for Evaluate and Review were added to the process (Shaun n.d.).

LEARNER-CENTRIC PREPLANNING

Learners must be involved in discussions in the preplanning stages. The teacher must give the learners a list of specific objectives and ask them what they already know about these objectives. This gives the teacher an idea of prior knowledge and misconceptions the learners already have (Clarke 2008). Clarke goes on to say that too many times, teachers have "missed opportunities to build on what pupils already know" (Clarke 2009, 72).

When learners are involved in the preplanning stages, they will be able to come up with ideas for contexts and activities to achieve their learning targets. This process assists teachers in planning for the occasions and triggers for instructional and learning tactic adjustments (Popham 2008).

The use of a learner-centric, standards-driven approach to planning will benefit the culture of the classroom as a place where assessment is a process from which teachers and learners can adjust what they are doing. Popham (2008, 95) contends (a) "substantial learning will occur for all students, irrespective of their academic aptitude"; (b) "students assume meaningful responsibility for their own learning and the learning of their classmates"; and (c) "formal and informal assessments generate data for informing adjustments to the teacher's instruction and the students' learning tactics."

In the three previous chapters, the processes of *Assessing, Evaluating,* and *Planning* were refocused to be learner-centric and standards-driven. This initiates a dynamic bond and reciprocal behaviors between teacher and learner, focused on the learning. In the next chapter, the final step of the Learner Improvement Cycle, *Learning* will be examined and focused on learner outcomes, not just teacher behaviors. This is a major shift in priority from examining teacher behaviors as the outcome to teacher behaviors being an input into learner outcomes.

Table 9.1. Teachers' Role in Planning in the Learner Improvement Cycle Continua

	Category	Beginning Teacher	Developing Teacher	Proficient Teacher	Advanced Teacher Meets All Criteria of Proficient, Plus
PLAN	Identify KPIs and cycle times	• Doesn't identify KPIs for effective unit planning • Doesn't identify KPIs for planning with learners using their assessment results.	• Begins to identify KPIs for backward-planning but does not align actions and time lines to achieve. • Begins to create process to plan with learners.	• Identify KPIs, actions, and cycle times of an effective unit planning process. • Identify KPIs, actions, and cycle times for planning with learners about their assessment results.	• Involves learners in the process of identifying KPIs, actions, and cycle times of effective unit planning. • Involves learners in the process of identifying KPIs, actions, and cycle times of effective planning with learners and their assessment results.
	Plans backward from evaluation of assessment	• Doesn't backward-plan from results of an assessment.	• Begins to use sources of input to backward-plan for learning.	• Plans and adapts resources, grouping, or instructional approaches for groups, and formatively assesses learners' progress in the learning progression for remediation, new teaching, or enrichment.	• Plans with learners and adapts resources or instructional approaches for individual, and formatively assesses learner's progress in the learning progression for remediation, new teaching, or enrichment.
	Creates a learner profile	• Is not sensitive to the development or background of individual learners.	• Has a system to collect minimal information on learners. • Makes stereotypical inferences based on this information.	• Creates a learner profile that includes information based on learners' development (physical, intellectual, emotional, social) and on their background (language, ethnicity, race, beliefs, socioeconomic status, experience).	• Monitors learner profile with a learner for developmental and environmental changes.

(continued)

Table 9.1. (*continued*)

	Category	Beginning Teacher	Developing Teacher	Proficient Teacher	Advanced Teacher Meets All Criteria of Proficient, Plus
PLAN	Use of results of assessments and qualitative learner feedback in planning	• Doesn't use results of pre-, formative, or summative assessment or learner feedback to plan instruction.	• Begins to use results of assessments to regroup learners, adapt resources, or teaching approach periodically.	• Uses results of assessments to regularly differentiate (content, process, and/ or product) for groups of learners (adapts resources, grouping or approaches).	• Uses results of assessments to differentiate and adapts resources, grouping, or approach with each learner.
DO	Writes appropriate learning target from the learning progression	• Doesn't have focused learning target. • Uses resources as the only curriculum instead of planning from the learning progression (text as curriculum).	• Posts a learning target that is tied to an activity, not the learning progression.	• Determines the appropriate learning target from a learning progression. • Writes a focused (audience, content, skill, performance, assessment) learning target for groups of learners that drives instruction for daily lesson or set of lessons in kid-friendly language.	• Works with learner to understand where the learning target aligns in the learning progression. • Writes a focused learning target with a learner that is individualized, student-friendly, aligns with content and skills, develops higher levels of thinking based on a taxonomy, and contains proficiency measures of assessment.

DO — Creating capacity matrices	• Doesn't have capacity matrices for learners to use for self-assessment.	• Begins to delineate learning target into the skills and knowledge learners need to master to be proficient to create a capacity matrix.	• Uses a teacher-created capacity matrix, aligned with rubric, which supports learning target.	• Collaborates with learners to create capacity matrices to track their progress in a learning progression.
Creating SMARTER goals and Individualized Learning Plans (ILP) from a learning progression	• Uses text to plan for instruction instead of a learning progression. • Makes no reference to having goals or learner involvement. • Creates no action plans in an ILP.	• References a learning progression and assessment results to plan for instruction but does not "unwrap" into prerequisite subskills. • Limits learner involvement to awareness of learning progression for goal setting. • Writes ILP actions that may not achieve the SMARTER goals.	• Knows how to use a learning progression and assessment results to unwrap a standard and identify prerequisite knowledge and skills needed. • Writes SMARTER goals for learners. • Writes ILPs to achieve SMARTER goals.	• Uses learning progression and assessment results to write SMARTER goals with learners. • Writes ILPs with learners to achieve SMARTER goals.
Learner involvement in lesson/unit planning	• Doesn't involve learners in feedback loops or unit/lesson planning process.	• Elicits general feedback from learners so feedback can be used in unit / lesson planning.	• Involves learners in planning process by soliciting specific feedback on processes/ content of lesson/unit.	• Involves learners in unit/ lesson planning process.

(continued)

Table 9.1. (continued)

	Category	Beginning Teacher	Developing Teacher	Proficient Teacher	Advanced Teacher Meets All Criteria of Proficient, Plus
DO	Use of collaborative inquiry planning	• Plans lessons alone and receives no feedback from colleagues or learners.	• Begins to share written lessons to receive feedback from colleagues or learners.	• Plans lessons with grade-level content partners and shares strategies for teaching groups of learners based on assessment data or learner feedback. • Posts lesson/unit plans on intranet/wiki to share with others.	• Plans lessons collaboratively with learners and posts on an intranet/wiki site for use by other teachers and learners.
	Planning relevance for learner, based on development, background, and interest	• Plans for an aggregate learner profile; doesn't take into account individual differences or experiences. • Doesn't plan relevance into curriculum or instruction for lessons.	• Begins to understand influences of development and background on learning and makes rudimentary attempts to plan for those differences. • Realizes that relevance is important and connects relevance in lessons for learners.	• Plans with learners, based on their development (physical, intellectual, emotional, social) and background (language, ethnicity, race, beliefs, socioeconomic status, experiences). • Plans activities with learners that are currently or collectively relevant.	• Makes learners aware of influences on their learning and assists learners in metacognitively planning for their learning. • Plans activities with each learner that are personally relevant to that learner.
CHECK	Checking the planning process	• Doesn't check KPIs on a regular cycle.	• Checks KPIs infrequently and doesn't monitor for refinement.	• Checks the planning process based on the KPIs in such a way that adjustments can be made.	• Has learners evaluate the effectiveness of the planning process through checking the KPIs.

CHECK	Checking SMARTER goals and ILPs	• Doesn't monitor creation or accuracy of SMARTER goals and ILP.	• Begins to develop a scoring guide for evaluating the quality of SMARTER goals and ILP.	• Checks to see if SMARTER goals have the components of effective SMARTER goals and action plan in the ILP will achieve the goals.	• Have learners create a scoring guide to evaluate accuracy of SMARTER goal and ILP.
	Aligning results of assessments with ILP	• Doesn't align results of assessment with goal-setting process or ILP.	• Begins to align results of assessment to SMARTER goals and ILPs.	• Checks to see that SMARTER goals based on learning targets and capacity matrices all align with the less-than-proficient results of assessments.	• Has learners check the alignment of SMARTER goals and capacity matrices with results of their assessments.
ADJUST	Adjusting planning process	• Doesn't refine planning process based on feedback.	• Begins to adjust planning process based on feedback received.	• Incorporates feedback into a refinement of planning process.	• Integrates learners into creation of new planning process.
	Adjusting teacher and learner plans	• Doesn't adjust ILP planning practices.	• Makes ineffective adjustments to ILPs that won't affect the KPIs.	• Adjusts ILP plans based on checking KPIs in a timely manner.	• Has learners adjust the ILP based on feedback from teachers and peers during the checking process.

(continued)

Table 9.1. *(continued)*

Suggested evidences:

- PDCA Plan with KPIs and cycle times
- Results of a collaborative protocol to analyze planning process
- Professional growth plan based on creating a planning process and results of planning
- Evidence of disaggregated data and effect on planning instruction
- Evidence of understanding of each learner's background and development and its impact on planning for learning
- Evidence of planning for the relevance of learners
- Learners' feedback on Plus/Deltas
- Posting collaboratively planned lessons and units on wiki/intranet

- Learner profile on each learner
- Evidence that learners can write an effective SMARTER goal
- Learner involvement in creating ILPs
- Learner uses the ILP to refine the adjustments to learning
- Focused (audience, content, skill, performance, assessment) learning target
- Placement of learning target in the learner progression
- Follow-through that ensures standards-based, backward-planning based on learners' results
- Capacity matrices created by learners to plan their learning and track their progress
- Monitoring of the KPIs of planning

PLANNING: CONVERSATIONS WITH THE STAKEHOLDERS

Voices of the Principals

Question: "How do you provide professional development for your staff in backward-planning, unwrapping standards, using data to inform instruction, differentiating instruction, and writing SMART goals?" Bill Stuckey described that his school staff engages in individual content meetings around backward-planning. He started with social studies in a three-day process: (a) "Day 1 agenda is identifying big ideas, enduring understandings, and unwrapping standards, (b) Day 2 deals with aligning performance tasks, and (c) Day 3 involves staff in daily planning."

Chris Benisch provides professional development to his staff on creating learning targets, gathering data, and using data to plan instruction by using this information in vertical teaming. Kelly Williams said these conversations happen in MAP meetings and are embedded into common plan time. These conversations involve what the data shows and identify kids in need of intervention.

Voices of the Teachers

Question: "How do you teach students how to goal-set for behavior and academics?" Robin Kietzmann says, "We do a lot of role playing during morning meeting for her third-grade group in which they set daily goals for the class. They have color-coded purple sheets for goal-setting. The students are a constant voice (in this process)." Kietzmann concluded with, "Goal setting is the premise for the community of your classroom." Janelle Stastny, who teams with Kietzmann, started with class goals on the shared vision, code of conduct, and self-direction and then moved to individual goals. The students set weekly goals for behavior and work ethic. She celebrates those who make their goals in class and sends the goal sheets home. Stastny says the students now remind each other to refocus. They want to help each other, especially because there is a reward if everyone meets their goal.

Anne Marie Dadley describes that it takes "a lot of direct instruction to set a good, specific goal." She recommended spending time up front and then following-through. She feels it will be better as students learn the system. She used the "5 Whys" tool to help students in understanding the reason for goal setting. Jennifer Rizzo modeled (the goal-setting process) "with a plus/delta chart and set class goals from that weekly review and graphed the results so students can see their progress." She modeled her own goals and plan about being back in school and giving 100 percent.

In setting goals for academics, Greg Russo describes that "when we're starting a new unit, we outline the essential questions, enduring understandings and learning targets. Students identify the goals, put them in their own words, and then put all that information in a capacity matrix and monitoring sheet." The preassessment or the end-of-unit assessment data-driven dialogue informs their goal-setting process. Those are the two systems to check and adjust learning.

Dadley says the goals for her students are also fed from the data-driven dialogue. "Then there is a razor-sharp focus for their goals and I set them loose. The students go find the resources, the students practice and determine when they are ready to take the postassessment. They are teaching themselves exactly what they need."

Jess Rapp describes three planning processes that empower students with personal ownership of their learning in her classroom: (a) students have a "yearly plan" that shows them all of the learning topics, practice assignments, and assessments for the entire course; (b) students complete individual long-term, weekly, and daily goal-setting; and (c) students have a process (flowchart) that requires them to use their material (books, notes, etc.) and personnel (peers, student-experts, etc.) resources prior to seeking help from the teacher. She feels that these three concepts also teach students the skills that every successful life-long learner has.

They also do a PCDA cycle about every other week. Students set weekly goals based on learning targets on which they have not yet achieved proficiency (plan), they create a list of strategies and steps they will take to meet their goals (do), they take the assessments (check), and then complete a data-driven dialogue, fixing any mistakes they might have made (adjust). Students regularly suggest how they should change and improve systems in the classroom on her class "parking lot." The parking lot has a plus (good things they see), delta (things they want to change, including suggestions for how to change it), questions (things they need to think about), and light bulbs (new ideas they can try).

Voices of the Students

Question: "How are you creating and monitoring goals based on the results of your assessments?" Students talked about the goal-setting process in their class. From the assessments, Penny says she gets a sheet of paper and writes her "goal" on it. On Friday, she puts "yes" or "no" and writes a new goal for the following week.

Maria says she sets two or three goals: "Some are for reading or math and some are for our behavior." Maria says students have to explain why they didn't meet their goal on the back of the sheet. Anna explains that she has a paper with "Goal Achievement" at the top. "It has three boxes of what we need to accomplish and how we are going to accomplish it."

As part of the planning process this year, students get to help one another more. Anna says, "Last year we didn't get to use peers, usually we had to ask the teacher." Maria concurs that "last year we didn't talk to students, we told the teachers we still need help on it and other students would say 'we don't want to do it again because we already know it.'" This year, the teachers are planning for flexible groupings in which the students are learning.

Penny states that "whoever got the same problems wrong, same as me, I would work with them and we would teach each other." Anna says that "sometimes the teachers don't get what we don't understand, because they know it. It's hard for them (the teachers). Peers know how you feel and can help you accomplish it."

Voices of the Parents

Question: "How are you involved in the goal-setting and action plans for your child's learning?" Parents report that students are becoming independent in their goal-setting process. The parents want to be a support for their student's goals and their learning. Jason Reynolds explained that "My daughter picks her goals. I'm a support for her goals." He further noticed her commitment to peer teaching as well. Last year, "when my daughter finished her homework, she used to go out and play; now she sits down and helps her sisters. I never requested this of her. I could have never convinced her to do that last year. No way."

Some parents, however, are finding out that the students are accomplishing their goals more on their own. Tomasita Perri said, "Sometimes I get jealous; when I ask my daughter if she needs help she said, 'No, I got it.'" Perri said, "Well I could . . ." but her daughter retorted, "Mom, I got it."

Key Points in Chapter 9:

1. How are learners involved in planning, which has traditionally been a teacher-driven activity?
   Once the learning targets have been identified, students collaborate with their teacher by writing their own individualized learning plan. Teachers must be aware of the Learner-Centered Principles from APA, as well as the student's background and development to advise their students in their goal-setting and planning.
2. How do we plan for the individual needs of learners through SMARTER goals?
   As students set their goals, they need to create their own continuous improvement process through the use of SMARTER goals. They write SMART goals that are specific, measureable, attainable, relevant, and time-bound. To these SMART goals, the students add the -ER to the process to "evaluate" and "review" their progress.

• *10* •

Learning: Learning in the Learner Improvement Cycle

Fundamental components of chapter 10:

- Teachers' and Learners' Role in Learning
- Learner-Centric Learning
- Teachers' and Learners' Roles in Teaching
- Learner-Centric Teaching
- Teacher's Role in Learning in the Learner Improvement Cycle Continua
- Teaching and Learning: Conversations with Stakeholders
- Key Points in Chapter 10

Guiding Questions in Chapter 10:

1. How do we transform our instructional system's focus away from teacher behaviors to teaching being the means to learning?
2. How do we move from a "pedagogy of poverty" to a "pedagogy of 'good teaching'"?
3. How do we help learners understand the connection between effort and success?

TEACHERS' AND LEARNERS' ROLES IN LEARNING

The time has come to shift the emphasis in American education from the teaching to the learning. The authors contend that the focal point should be on the learning, and the teaching is the vehicle to accomplish this. Notice the Learner Improvement Cycle chart (see Figure Sect 4.1) and its spotlight on learning; with this approach, teaching becomes the means to the end. For too many years, educators have dissected the act of teaching into its component parts, expecting that if teaching is done properly, then learning should occur. This chapter will not be more of the same. The focus of *this* chapter will be on behaviors, of both teacher and student, that have a positive effect on learning.

The results, currently being achieved in education today, challenge the premise that teachers can educate our young alone. The authors would also argue that past research tends to concentrate only on the results of classrooms that are teacher-directed. In a learner-centric, standards-driven model, learners are considered teaching resources for others as well as partners in their own learning. More research needs to be designed to measure the results in a learner-centric environment.

Marzano Research Laboratories has conducted a study that correlates the results of students in schools that are a part of the ReInventing Schools Coalition (RISC). The ReInventing Schools Coalition embodies a learner-centric, standards-driven model and has been implementing this model for the past fifteen years. The study compared the odds of a student scoring proficient or above at a RISC school compared to the odds of a student scoring proficient or above at a non-RISC school for reading, writing, and mathematics. The level of implementation of the model was taken into consideration. Table 10.1 shows the encouraging data:

Table 10.1.   Chances of Being Proficient in a RISC School vs. Non-RISC School

Subject	RISC vs. Non-RISC Schools	High-Implementation RISC vs. Non-RISC Schools
Reading	2.3:1	5.1:1
Writing	2.5:1	4.7:1
Math	2.4:1	2.7:1

So, the more a learner-centric, standards-driven model is implemented with fidelity, the better the chances students have of being proficient. Robert Marzano is currently creating a version of his *Art and Science of Teaching* (2007) for District 50 that now cites learner evidences of implementation in addition to the teacher evidences.

Traditional schooling has sapped the energy out of learning. Currently, educators have controlled the classroom to the point that all learning is directed through the teacher. Learners have very little say about the manner in which they learn, how they will show what they know and can do, and from whom they will learn. If learning is defined as the change in attitude, thought, or behavior as a result of an experience (Ormrod 2004), then the classroom must be designed to allow learners to learn from a wider variety of people and experiences. They must be able to learn from one another, from their teacher, and from the wider world.

The reader will note that at the advanced end of the learning continua, the criteria outline what educators need to do to move toward an essential-progressivist philosophy. Within each continuum is a set of tools, knowledge, and skills to support teachers moving in this direction. These tools and processes provide teachers the avenue for learners to use their voice to define learner-centric classrooms.

LEARNER-CENTRIC LEARNING

In order to create a school culture where all learners are expected to be proficient or better, teachers must leverage learners to partner with them. This means teachers will have to teach students how to be learners and partners. This can be accomplished through teaching learners how to use tools to:

(a) define what they want their classroom to be,
(b) explain what everyone will need to do to accomplish this vision in different environments,
(c) assume responsibility for their own learning (gradual release of responsibility),
(d) understand and actuate the Learner Improvement Cycle through setting, monitoring, and evaluating their academic and behavioral goals,
(e) adjust learning tactics, if needed, and learn to advocate for what they need, and
(f) find audiences and resources to authenticate learning.

Shared Vision

In a learner-centric classroom, the teacher and learners define what they want their classroom to become. Using the shared vision of the district and the school, the learners will brainstorm and prioritize descriptors that align what the learners jointly agree will be the classroom vision (Delorenzo et al. 2009). The common moral purpose of the classroom will influence the shared vision.

In Adams County School District 50, the district vision is (a) preparing learners for the twenty-first century, (b) nurturing a love of learning and inquiry, and (c) celebrating the diversity in the community. A first-grade classroom translated this district vision into a classroom shared vision of "Work hard, be nice, respect each other and the environment."

Set of Learning Guidelines

Learners will then need to establish specific criteria of what everyone will need to do to accomplish this shared vision in their classroom and throughout the school (Delorenzo et al. 2009). Learners will list all the venues in their learning *environment* where they will make their shared vision come true. Venues could include the classroom, the media center, hallways, bathrooms, playground, and so on. Learners will then focus on how to make the shared vision come alive in these environments. Learners might define what working hard or being nice would look like in the classroom, the media center, the hallway, and on the playground.

Gradual release of responsibility. Previously, some learners were asked to assume responsibility for their own learning through the gradual release of support in a teacher-directed classroom. This was summarized as, "I do, we do, you do together and then you do alone" (Fisher and Frey 2008, 4). (See Figure 10.1.)

This implies that the teacher's responsibility shifts to the learner responsibility as the teacher has the knowledge and models the learning for the learner in a focus lesson and then provides an opportunity for guided practice. Learners then are encouraged to collaborate before independently demonstrating their learning.

Marzano's four-part rubric (scoring guide) (2007, 21) implies a more learner-centric focus than the previous model. Students are provided the focus lesson only if they need the instruction based on the results of the preassessment. His model is portrayed with a score 1 = you do with help, score 2 = you do the simple parts, score 3 = you do the simple and complex, and score 4 = you take it beyond the way you were taught or explain to someone else. This model focuses much more on the learner behaviors and the teacher facilitating learners' behaviors. (See Figure 10.2.)

Figure 10.1. The Gradual Release of Responsibility to the Student

The four-point scoring guide that is being used in District 50:

Table 10.2. Marzano's Four-Point Rubric (2007, 21)

Score 4 Advanced	In addition to exhibiting level 3 performance, the learner's responses demonstrate *in-depth inferences and applications that go beyond what was taught in class.*
Score 3 Proficient	The learner's responses demonstrate no major errors or omissions regarding *any of the simple and complex information and/or processes (THAT WERE EXPLICITLY TAUGHT).*
Score 2 Partially Proficient	The learner's responses indicate major errors or omissions regarding the more complex ideas and processes; however, they do not indicate major errors or omissions relative to the *simpler details* and processes.
Score 1 Emerging	The learner provides responses that indicate a distinct lack of understanding of the knowledge. However, *with help,* the learner demonstrates partial understanding of some of the knowledge.
Score 0 Unsatisfactory	The learner provides little or no response. Even with help, the learner *does not exhibit a partial understanding of the knowledge.*

The Learner Improvement Cycle and Goal-Setting

In the previous three chapters, the authors outlined the learner involvement in assessing, evaluating, and planning. In this chapter, the learners must understand and actuate their part of the Learner Improvement Cycle. Teachers must be willing to transfer control to the learner through goal-setting and teach learners how to partner in their own learning. In order for the teacher to have time to collaborate with each learner to monitor their goals, the teacher will have to plan a unit ahead of the fastest learner in the class.

Learners must follow the shared vision of the classroom, follow the learner-created code of conduct, and be able to work and advocate for their needs as they learn the targets/objectives that they must master. The goals must focus on what the learner needs to learn, not on what the teacher covers.

To this end, the learner must know what they need to know and do to be proficient or advanced on the learning targets/objectives. They need to use the capacity matrix that breaks down the skills and knowledge to build their learning. The learners will then create goals in a PDCA process in order to accomplish those goals. In a learner-centric classroom, learners must set, monitor, and evaluate their academic and behavioral goals.

For academic goals, during the planning process, learners will set the goals based on the results of the preassessing, evaluating, and planning phases of the cycle. Learners will then use their capacity matrices to monitor their progress in achieving proficiency. Teachers will validate the evidence that the learner uses to show proficiency and provide additional resources if additional learning is needed. If the teacher and learner agree that the learner has met their goals, they collaboratively set new goals.

For behavioral goals, learners can reference their guidelines for learning behavior and then set classroom or individual goals. These can be written in terms of the personal social learning targets/objectives. If a learner is unable to adhere to the code of conduct, then it can also be written as a behavioral goal that the learner is expected to achieve. These can also be monitored through capacity matrices and depend on the teacher and learner partnering in their achievement.

The learners will include the resources, groups, and approaches on their PDCA plans that they will need to accomplish learning. These resources can include time with the teacher in direct instruction in a large group, small groups, or one-on-one. It could also mean using learner experts in the room who have already mastered the learning targets/objectives. The learner will determine how they will demonstrate their learning once their plan is accomplished.

Adjusting Tactics and Advocacy

With a common moral purpose, which all learners need to reach the proficient level or better, learners may find that they need to adjust their learning tactics in order to accomplish their goals. Learners will need to advocate for what they need. In a learner-centric classroom, where a learning community has been nurtured and the class has created a culture where trust and collective efficacy is evident, learners will feel comfortable telling the teacher (and peers, if they so choose) when they need help to meet the target/objective. The learner and the teacher will collaborate on additional resources and support to help the learner be successful.

Real-World Audiences

As learners begin to complete their goals and learning targets/objectives, it is important to find an authentic audience, where appropriate, to give learners feedback to authenticate their learning in context. This provides real-world relevance and feedback to learners against a public standard (Darling-Hammond, Ancess, and Falk 1995). If professionals, who have a vested interest in the student learning, can help write a rubric using a public standard, the learner will get invaluable feedback of how the real world works. Not all learnings will have an appropriate authentic audience, and in these cases, learners will present their learning to peers and their teacher.

TEACHERS' AND LEARNERS' ROLES IN TEACHING

Good Teaching

If what is expected is *proficiency for all,* then good learner-centric pedagogy must be in place to support this learning. As far back as 1991, Haberman did extensive research on urban settings and found that what people described as good teaching was in fact a pedagogy of poverty. The pedagogy of poverty is defined by a core of teaching strategies as:

Table 10.3. Attributes of the Pedagogy of Poverty

Giving information	Reviewing tests
Asking questions	Assigning homework
Giving directions	Reviewing homework
Making assignments	Settling disputes
Monitoring seatwork	Punishing noncompliance
Reviewing assignments	Marking papers
Giving tests	Giving grades

(Haberman 1991)

This is how most people were taught and describes what most people today think of as teaching. Haberman goes on to say that the reason this pedagogy appeals to people is because they rely on what they know instead of thoughtful analysis of the options that could be possible to educate all learners for the twenty-first century. Some people don't know there are any other options. He says this poverty pedagogy appeals to others because they have low expectations for and fear minorities and the poor. They think these populations are best served by being told what to do, think, and learn. This pedagogy of poverty does not work. Children who are educated under this system are not ready for the workplace or postsecondary options. The authors would suggest that current reforms are trying to perfect this pedagogy of poverty instead of designing a new educational system for all learners. This new system needs to better match the way learners naturally learn what society has defined they should learn (the standards).

Haberman (1991) suggests that when good teaching is going on, whether for children of poverty or not, students are involved in their learning through real-life experiences, working with other learners in heterogeneous groups, and in accessing technology to gain information. He says learners must be involved in activities that are relevant such as:

(a) exploring issues they regard as vital;
(b) explaining human differences;
(c) helping to see major concepts and not engaging in the pursuit of isolated facts;
(d) applying ideals such as fairness, equity, or justice;
(e) thinking about an idea that questions common assumptions and relates new ideas to previously learned ideas; and
(f) reflecting on their own lives and why they have come to believe as they do.

The final assumption of good teaching is that learners are given the opportunity to redo, polish, or perfect their work because it is *the process* that allows them to excel. Haberman's work sets the tone for a redefinition of good teaching in the classroom. Haberman's thinking leads to a desire to search for a learner-centric pedagogy. This has led to the results-driven, research-based strategies of Marzano (2007) and Delorenzo et al. (2009).

LEARNER-CENTRIC TEACHING

Knowing the Learners

The teacher's role is to set up the conditions for this learner-centric teaching to occur. This means the teacher must release control to the learners and know and understand each of the learners. Marzano's research (2007) indicates teacher's positive interactions with learners increase the students' learning. He suggests that learning about the learners' interests and lives shows that the teacher cares about the learners, in addition to their learning. Delorenzo et al. (2009, 74) concur that teachers must understand their learners—"their learning needs, their goals, their interests, and their unique learning styles."

Resource for Deep Knowledge

The teacher needs to be one of the resources for deep knowledge acquisition for the learner (Marzano 2007). This will happen through ensuring there is a guaranteed, viable curriculum, organized into learning progressions, based on standards that are connected to the learners' prior and future learning. The instruction will then flow from the standards to be learned (Delorenzo et al. 2009).

The teacher may have to do some direct instruction while the learner is acquiring background knowledge in order to access the current learning. This will require the teacher to provide a gradual release of support and allow for differentiation of content, process, and product (Tomlinson 2000) as well as individualize the pacing.

Facilitating Learning and Questioning Strategies

Students' learning is accomplished through the relationships they have with their peers and their teacher (Marzano 2007). This is partially accomplished through the teacher supporting learning and behavior so that the students feel their teacher is a teammate in their learning. Delorenzo et al. (2009) believe this is through two-way communication and learning rather than the teacher being the source of all instruction. Teachers become the facilitators of learning.

As teachers realize they are not the only resource available to learners, the teacher needs to create a system to recognize learner experts. The learner experts, who have already mastered this learning, can serve as another effective facilitator of learning.

Questioning is a powerful tool to help learners understand what is important, how to organize their thinking, and engage in their learning (Fisher and Frey 2007; Marzano 2003). Constructing effective and authentic higher-level questions, based on a taxonomy, can engage learners in critical thinking. It can encourage learners to think at higher levels and teachers to check for understanding and learning. Learners must be taught how to raise the level of thinking in the questions they design for themselves and peers, which will take their learning beyond the teacher-directed curriculum.

Connecting Past, Present, and Future Learning

Teachers then become the facilitators of students connecting the current learning targets/objectives to previous learning. Teachers need to understand the learning progression and the students' background knowledge in order to make the current learning relevant. This helps students engage in new learning as they activate their previous schemas and integrate the new learning. This strategy teaches students how to describe why they are learning what they are learning.

Increasing Learner Voice

In a learner-centric classroom, learners' voices must be legitimized by the teacher processing the feedback given by the learners. By using tools and processes to allow learners a vehicle for continuously improving the classroom, the teacher validates that this is the learners' classroom as well. The teacher must then take the input and change the classroom conditions based on that feedback.

Enrichment and Reteaching

Using learners' results can continually increase the quality of the learning environment. An ongoing data-driven dialogue, based on the results of classroom performance assessments and the learners' capacity matrices, can focus the teacher and learner on the current needs of the learner.

If the results indicate learner proficiency has not been met, then the teacher must support relearning until proficient learning occurs. If learners have met proficiency, then students can extend their learning into knowledge utilization (decision making, problem solving, and experimenting [Marzano and Kendall 2008, 4]) inside the classroom or move from the classroom into the community on that concept. This would document a score four (4) or "advanced" (Marzano 2007) and move the learner onto the next concept.

Increasing Motivation and Effort

These learner-centric strategies are very motivational to students and increase engagement in the class as students realize they are in charge of their learning. The teacher needs to continually reinforce the connection between the learners' effort and their achievement to ensure they maintain their internal locus of control (Marzano 2007).

Celebrating Learning

According to Eaker, DuFour, and Burnette (2002), celebrations should happen in a timely fashion and reinforce the vision, values, and achievement results of the organization. Recognition should be given to individuals and collective groups. It is important to develop ceremonies to recognize high performance as well as celebrate improvement.

At the conclusion of chapter 10, the reader sees the teacher's role shift from a focus on teaching to learning. Gone are the days when learners complete a unit of study, receive their grades, and move on to the next unit whether they've mastered the material early or needed more time. In a learner-centric classroom, students stay with the learning long enough to be proficient or advanced. That means time becomes the variable; learning is the constant. It is up to the adults and the learners in the system to utilize tools and processes in the classroom to accomplish the learning.

In learner-centric schools, schooling and learning become much more aligned for the learner. Schools are no longer places where students lose their love of learning and inquiry. Instead, they learn to be in control of their own learning process and support the learning of others. Learners are empowered to plan their own goals from assessments and gather resources to accomplish their goals. The teacher and their peers become just one of the myriad of resources for the student to use to accomplish their learning.

In chapter 11, the authors will lead the reader through a review of the enduring understandings of the book and propose a national conversation that would focus on systemic learner-centric change that would represent reawakening the learner in all public schools. This may be the final chance to reform public education. In 2014, the goals of NCLB will culminate and the question will be, "Are all our children proficient?"

Table 10.4. Teacher's Role in Learning in the Learner Improvement Cycle Continua

	Category	Beginning Teacher	Developing Teacher	Proficient Teacher	Advanced Teacher Meets All Criteria of Proficient, Plus
PLAN	Identifying KPIs and cycle times for learning	• Doesn't identify KPIs for effective learning. • Doesn't involve learners in determining KPIs for learning.	• Begins to identify KPIs for learning but does not align actions and time lines to achieve. • Begins to create process to partner with learners to ensure their learning.	• Identifies KPIs, actions and cycle times for effective learning. • Partners with learners to define the criteria for proficient or advanced learning.	• Involves learners in their inclusion in the process of identifying KPIs, actions, and cycle times of effective learning. • Refines exemplars for each proficiency level. • Shortens the cycle times to measure proficiency.
	Planning for gradual release of support	• Plans for a teacher-directed classroom.	• Begins to release learning to student.	• Provides for class gradual release of support (I do, we do, you do together, you do).	• Provides individual release of support for learner (I do, we do, you do together, you do).
DO	Connecting to past, present, and future learning	• Doesn't connect previous or future learning to present learning targets for student.	• Connects present learning to previous learning.	• Facilitates students connecting present learning to previous learning. • Prepares learners for future learning targets. • Teaches learners how to describe why they are learning what they are learning.	• Guides learner to see connection between past, present, and future learning targets.

DO				
Using learner-centric pedagogy	• Doesn't use student learning styles or teach in a learner-centric manner.	• Begins to see benefit of students owning their own learning through learner-centric strategies and tries strategies in their lesson plans.	• Teaches in a learner-centric mode most of time giving learners a voice in the classroom and uses student learning styles. • Relinquishes control of the class and becomes a resource for learning.	• Creates an environment where student-to-student interaction focuses on things that are important to the learner. • Builds capacity in learners for both learner-centric content and process. • Creates conditions for learners to serve as resources for one another.
Improving learner engagement	• Doesn't involve students in their learning process. Teacher *only* tells, lectures, or demonstrates. • Engages learners passively.	• Begins to ask students questions to extract knowledge. • Facilitates and guides instructional activities that engage students in their learning, ritualistically.	• Engages learners in hands-on, relevant, challenging, and interactive lessons. • Helps learners identify which teaching strategies best fit their learning styles. • Displays passion for their subject AND for their learners. • Collaborates with learners to engage them through their knowledge, skills, and individualized goal-setting and planning.	• Engages learners in the real-life human themes. • Identifies and utilizes learner experts to allow learners to become teachers. • Constructs opportunities for peer-and reciprocal teaching. • Uses technology to access information.

(continued)

Table 10.4. *(continued)*

	Category	Beginning Teacher	Developing Teacher	Proficient Teacher	Advanced Teacher Meets All Criteria of Proficient, Plus
DO	Using questioning strategies	• Doesn't teach learners how to generate their own questions beyond the lower levels of a taxonomy.	• Develops capacity in learner to develop questions in all levels of a taxonomy.	• Provides ways for learners to apply multiple levels of questions and tasks that stimulate their thinking beyond teacher-driven curriculum.	• Teaches learners to generate their own levels of questions and tasks so learners facilitate student-to-student demonstrations of learning.
	Improving learning behaviors	• Doesn't create clear expectations for learner behavior.	• Enforces teacher-created classroom and school rules autocratically.	• Involves learners in creation of a set of guidelines for classroom behaviors. • Holds students accountable for an environment that is conducive to learning.	• Delegates the creation of a set of guidelines in classroom to students; learners hold each other accountable for an environment that is conducive to learning.
CHECK	Checking KPIs on cycles	• Doesn't check KPIs on a regular cycle.	• Checks KPIs infrequently and doesn't monitor for refinement.	• Checks the learning process based on the KPIs in such a way that adjustments can be made.	• Has students evaluate the effectiveness of their learning process through checking the KPIs.

Aligning effort and achievement	• Doesn't assist learners in making connection between effort and reaching proficiency. • Provides learners with extrinsic rewards for good work.	• Teaches learners to understand cause and effect relationship between effort and reaching proficiency. • Moves toward reinforcing internal locus of control for learners.	• Builds capacity in learners to see connection between their effort and success in being proficient by graphing indicators of effort with proficiency. • Reinforces internal locus of control for learners.	• Builds students' self-awareness of what is successful learning. • Assists learners in using their strengths to compensate for their weaknesses.
Utilizing learning results	• Tells learners what they've learned that day.	• Closes lesson by telling learners what they've learned and students provide evidence of that learning.	• Teaches learners to independently communicate to teacher what they now know and are able to do. • Challenges learners to redo, polish, and perfect their work based on feedback.	• Provides authentic audiences for learners to communicate what they now know and are able to do. • Evaluates learning by a public standard.
Creating a feedback loop during instruction	• Doesn't monitor guided or independent practice for error patterns.	• Checks for understanding during lesson but does not monitor for errors during guided or independent practice.	• Checks for understanding, provides and monitors guided or independent practice for mastery. • Creates a flowchart process for students to find resources or clarify learning to use during guided or independent practice.	• Gives opportunity for learners to create their own flowchart to gain and receive feedback from teacher and other students during their learning.

CHECK

(continued)

Table 10.4. *(continued)*

	Category	Beginning Teacher	Developing Teacher	Proficient Teacher	Advanced Teacher Meets All Criteria of Proficient, Plus
CHECK	Creating a feedback loop for assignments or assessments	• Doesn't give or know how to give learners timely, specific feedback on their work (just a percentage of right or wrong). • Doesn't assist learners in knowing why they committed errors. • Gives assignments without expectations or rubrics. • Averages grades; however, learners can't explain proficiency on standards.	• Begins to provide feedback but is not specific or immediate. • Gives assignments and provides a rubric. • Assigns grades and learners begin to understand link between assignments and standards.	• Provides learners with specific, descriptive, frequent, constructive, and immediate feedback on their work. • Provides a rubric and exemplars of work on each assignment. • Involves learners in self-assessment of progress on standards and goal-setting.	• Teaches learners how to self-assess and provide feedback to peers on their work that is specific, descriptive, frequent, constructive, and immediate. • Teaches learners to advocate for themselves when mastery of learning target is not accomplished. • Involves learners in creation of rubric and selection of exemplars. • Teaches learners how to monitor own progress on standards and justify how they met proficiency or better standard.
ADJUST	Adjusting based on the checking the KPIs	• Doesn't refine learning process based on monitoring KPIs.	• Begins to adjust learning process based on data gathered from KPIs.	• Partners with students to refine learning practices based on data.	• Integrates students into refining their own learning practices independently. • Shortens cycle times.

ADJUST				
Differentiating instruction	• Covers material and teaches to middle of class. • Doesn't differentiate for learners' needs.	• Recognizes need for differentiation but does not monitor and regroup based on learners' feedback.	• Adjusts instruction based on regular feedback from *the learners* (specific, descriptive, frequent, constructive, and immediate). • Makes adjustment process transparent to learners. • Varies resources, groupings, and approaches to meet *groups* of learners' needs.	• Adjusts instruction based on feedback from *each learner.* • Varies resources, grouping, and approach based on the *individual learner's* advocacy.
Providing enrichment and reteaching	• Has learners who do not know their level of competence. • Continues to teach without responding to various levels of learner competence.	• Bases determination of what skills and knowledge need to be enriched, continued to be learned, or retaught on the checking of KPIs.	• Bases the determination of what skills and knowledge need to be enriched, continued to be learned, or retaught on requested *learner* feedback.	• Creates avenues for enrichment, continued learning, or being retaught based on learner advocacy.
Celebrating learning	• Doesn't celebrate learning progress or accomplishments.	• Does not match magnitude of celebration to magnitude of learning accomplished.	• Celebrates learning with internal stakeholders only.	• Creates celebration ceremonies with all stakeholders, especially involving learners in the planning of the celebration.

(continued)

Table 10.4. *(continued)*

Suggested evidences:

- PDCA plans with KPIs and cycle times
- Observed lessons are error-free for content and interdisciplinary connections
- Evidence of the use of a guaranteed viable curriculum
- Learner-created set of learning behavior guidelines for classroom
- Improved learning toward proficiency
- Learner-created rubrics for content
- Learner-created flowcharts for classroom processes
- Lesson plans adjusted based on learner and teacher feedback
- Learner exemplars
- Documentation of individual support to learners
- Evidence of specific feedback to learners
- Documentation of learner-centric environments from classroom walk-throughs and informal or formal observations
- Evidence that learners can plan projects that are relevant to them
- Evidence that learners understand levels of questioning

- Standards-driven grading, tracking systems, and reports
- Monitoring plan for supervising teaching practices
- Observed lessons document the process of gradual release of support
- Monitoring sheets for guided and independent practice
- Evidence that learning meets a public standard
- Matrix of teachers' strengths to be used for recommending staff modeling
- Showing examples in newsletters/faculty weekly announcements of where effective teaching is getting results
- Objectives/learning targets for meetings that the principal facilitates to model good teaching practices
- Staff development plan for effective research-based teaching practices
- Plan for celebration of effort and learning to proficiency
- Evidence of celebrations of learning

LEARNING: CONVERSATIONS WITH THE STAKEHOLDERS

Voices of the Principals

Question: "How have you observed evidence from teachers and students that your school has an effective learning cycle in place?" Chris Benisch discussed that as a result of vertical team meetings, they now graph the prepost test data each month and have conversations about rigor and topics such as identifying the criteria for a good sentence and paragraph. They look at work samples from grades K–5 to see the progression, which has a nice tier to it. They even put exemplars of student work in their trophy case! Benisch concluded that right now they have anecdotes and are working to align their practices.

Sarah Gould added that the teacher-evaluation system will need to reflect the expectations for teacher learning. Her teachers came with a PDCA and capacity matrix for their own learning. Benisch finished with, "Once we start getting actual results, our celebrations will need to be more transparent."

Voices of the Teachers

Question: "How do you move practice from the teacher-directed to more learner-centric teaching strategies?" Jess Rapp describes how in class she has a myriad of teaching strategies: they do large-group instruction, small-group instruction, teacher-driven groups, student-expert driven groups, groups in which all students (no matter their proficiency) take a turn leading the group, computer-based tutorials, and any other strategy that students may suggest.

Greg Russo says, "You have to give up being the center of attention. It's tough to give up." The transition for him was once you are doing the standards-based idea; kids are working at their own pace. Once they are working at their own pace, you have to differentiate. "Now I spend my time getting resources that they can access: videos, materials, and recording myself in ten-minute chunks when they are ready for it. In the past I would do whole group, and maybe only ten would be ready for it. It was such a huge waste of time, for both of us. All of that energy I was putting into these awesome lectures. Now I still get to teach the kids, but now it's when they are ready for it. In a small group, I'll sit down with them, guide them through it, the kids will videotape it and put it on the computer, like you are cloning yourself around the room."

Next, teachers responded to: "What teaching strategies are you using to accomplish *proficiency for all?*" Rapp describes the process where those who aren't proficient overall follow up the error-analysis process with extra practice sessions. "Extra practice sessions are typically small, cooperative groups, working together on a learning target until they feel confident in their abilities to achieve proficiency." "Expert students" sometimes serve as tutor-leaders for small groups that need more assistance. Once students feel confident in their ability to pass an assessment, they may retake (an alternate version) of the assessment.

The teachers responded to the question, "How are you making the connection between student effort and student success overt for the student?" One strategy was to ask the kids.

Janelle Stastny asks her kids who have had success or a lack of success, "What did you do?" On testing, they could identify strategies that they used to be more successful. If they didn't score well, she asked the students what they could've done differently. Another strategy was defining effort and/or designing an effort rubric. Stastny has her students define what effort means as an activity.

Greg Russo has "effort" on his capacity matrices so students make the connection between effort and achievement. He wants them to make the connection that if they put a lot of effort and get advanced, or on the flip side if they put in a tremendous amount of effort and are not doing well, then they are able to reflect on what's going on.

Rapp, Russo's teammate, has students use a daily monitoring sheet, where they graph their academic achievement side-by-side with their effort. She calls students up to conference with them about the connection between their effort and achievement. The visual nature of a graph makes it easy for them to make connections.

VOICES OF THE LEARNERS

Question: "How do you give feedback to your teacher to check and adjust their instruction?" Anna was the first to answer. She said, "We have this chart at school. Our teacher leaves the room, and we put ideas on a sticky note of what went well, what needs to be improved, what questions we have." She would return and respond to the sticky notes. Sometimes she does what the students ask. "Last year, the teacher ignored us and did it her way. I know my teacher cares and she will help us on that subject." In another class, Penny describes that they sit in groups in a meeting, talk, and the teacher will do something about it.

Voices of the Parents

Question: "What kind of training do parents need to understand the teaching/learning process so they can reinforce learning at home?" Parents felt other parents needed more information about what District 50's standards-based system is and how to understand the teaching/learning process so they can reinforce it at home. They all thought that mailing a DVD home to all district patrons is an excellent idea.

Jason Reynolds said he would watch the DVD together with his daughter and then email the teacher with any questions. They also agreed that more use of the e-mail would be a low-cost way to share information. Jason concluded that he felt and has seen a difference in the teachers this year. They are getting to know the parents, and it has brought the community together.

Key Points in Chapter 10:

1. How do we transform our instructional system's focus away from teacher behaviors to teaching being the means to learning?

   The teacher needs to develop a learning environment where the learners have an active voice in the classroom through developing a shared vision and the behavioral guidelines for learning. The learners collaborate with the teacher in the Learner Improvement Cycle and take responsibility for the accomplishments of their goals. The teacher becomes a facilitator and a resource for the learning.

2. How do we move from a "pedagogy of poverty" to a "pedagogy of 'good teaching'"?

   Teaching needs to transform from a very teacher-directed learning environment to one in which the teacher knows the learners well and facilitates their learning, remediation, and enrichment by increasing the student voice. Haberman believes that instead of learning isolated facts, students need to be engaged in real-world issues such as exploring human differences, applying ideals, questioning common assumptions, and reflecting on their own lives.

3. How do we help learners understand the connection between effort and success?

   As learners become more in charge of their learning, they will understand the connection between their effort and their increased learning. They will have more of an internal locus of control.

Section 5

WIDE AWAKE IN THE TWENTY-FIRST CENTURY: PROFICIENCY FOR ALL

I will not sleep through my education.

—Bart Simpson

Fundamental components of section 5:

- Setting the Alarm for a Wake-Up Call
- Gap Analysis Chart to a Twenty-First-Century Learner-Centric, Standards-Driven Educational System

SETTING THE ALARM FOR A WAKE-UP CALL

Bart Simpson doesn't want to sleep through his education and neither do the rest of America's children. What is the alarm clock we need to set to wake everybody up and who should set that alarm clock?

Table Sect 5.1 has been prepared to guide the reader to the conclusion that actuating the component of the chapters of this book will lead a school community to competent, confident learners prepared for the twenty-first century. In addition, if adult stakeholders are feeling committed and satisfied in continuously improving their practice, then the school and stakeholders will be on the right track to creating a *proficiency for all* system that is learner-centric and standards-driven.

Mid-course adjustments may be necessary if learners and adults of the school community are expressing feelings or acting in ways that demonstrate dissatisfaction with current practices. In using the table, stakeholders can diagnose problems within the system, based on the current emotional reactions of the members of the community. In examining the reactions in the first two columns, mid-course adjustments could point to issues and solutions delineated in certain chapters of this book. For instance, if the learners are "dazed and confused" and the adults are "random and resistive," the necessary "check and adjust" would be to identify or clarify a common moral purpose. The research supporting the process to accomplish a common moral purpose is found in chapter 3. The "plan, do, check, and adjust" (PCDA) process is outlined in the continua at the end of the chapter, with suggested evidences.

These components must be prioritized. To begin the process would involve creating a culture for change. It is critical to begin with developing a shared vision for your organization that unites the staff and learners under a common moral purpose. Next, the stakeholders of the school need to develop the culture in which the school is ready for change, creating a trusting environment to doubt current practices and understand and behave in a manner that collectively they realize they are stronger by working together. The final component to be addressed, if all others are in place, is determining the change to be undertaken. In this case, the change is developing a partnership with learners in the Learner Improvement Cycle.

Table Sect 5.1. Gap Analysis Chart to a Twenty-First Century, Learner-Centric, Standards-Driven Educational System

If the Learners Are Feeling...	If the Adults Are Feeling...	On-track (Checks and Adjustments)	CULTURE for CHANGE				THE CHANGE			
Competent and confident to be successful in the twenty-first century	Satisfied and committed to a new continuously improving system		Common Moral Purpose	Readiness for Change	Trust-to-Doubt	Collective Efficacy	Assessing	Evaluating	Planning	Learning
Dazed and Confused	Random and Resistive		Missing? See chapter 3	Readiness for change	Trust-to-doubt	Collective efficacy	Assessing	Evaluating	Planning	Learning
Passive and Compliant	Unprepared and Fearful		Common moral purpose	Missing? See chapter 4	Trust-to-doubt	Collective efficacy	Assessing	Evaluating	Planning	Learning
Unempowered and Disconnected	Cynical and Skeptical		Common moral purpose	Readiness for change	Missing? See chapter 5	Collective efficacy	Assessing	Evaluating	Planning	Learning
Powerless and Fatalistic	"Silo-ed" and Unfulfilled		Common moral purpose	Readiness for change	Trust-to-doubt	Missing? See chapter 6	Assessing	Evaluating	Planning	Learning
Pre- and Formative → Unaware Summative → Unrewarded			Common moral purpose	Readiness for change	Trust-to-doubt	Collective efficacy	Missing? See chapter 7	Evaluating	Planning	Learning
Error-Laden and Apathetic	Nonreflective and Scattered		Common moral purpose	Readiness for change	Trust-to-doubt	Collective efficacy	Assessing	Missing? See chapter 8	Planning	Learning
Uninformed and Disengaged	Unstructured and Serendipitous		Common moral purpose	Readiness for change	Trust-to-doubt	Collective efficacy	Assessing	Evaluating	Missing? See chapter 9	Learning
Bored and Ignorant	Ineffective and Frustrated		Common moral purpose	Readiness for change	Trust-to-doubt	Collective efficacy	Assessing	Evaluating	Planning	Missing? See chapter 10

Moving from Sleepwalking to Reawakening the Learner

Fundamental components of chapter 11:

- Call to Action!
- Key Point of Reawakening the Learner

Review of the Essential Question:

How does our society create schools to ensure *proficiency for all* learners to meet the ever-changing needs of the twenty-first century?

CALL TO ACTION!

Based on a review of current research and experiences of stakeholders currently in public education, the authors have created a framework for school personnel to begin defining what learner-centric, standards-driven practices could mean in their school.

Public education must undergo a transformation to accomplish *proficiency for all* learners. The current system society has clung to for the last hundred years was intended to meet a very different outcome. An educational system based on an agrarian, industrial model was intended to provide access and proficiency for some students.

Now, in an age where society is demanding *proficiency for all* learners, educators are trying to accomplish this goal within the old system. The current public-education institution will not reach the new goal of *proficiency for all*. A

171

new educational system should be built around the following understandings to reawaken the learner:

1. Organizational moral purpose must align to *proficiency for all*. Each individual coming to an organization brings her own moral purpose and it's up to the principalship to assist each stakeholder in reflecting and stating her own moral purpose for educating our youth. Then the principalship must bring all these individual moral purposes into consensus to create a common moral purpose. A common moral purpose must center on a philosophy that espouses *proficiency for all*. No longer does our society, in the twenty-first century, have jobs available for graduates who are not proficient. This may challenge our society to prepare itself for a thinking, proficient workforce and citizenry.

2. School culture must be restructured to satisfy the new expectations of *proficiency for all*. The processes that need to be in place for the revision of this school culture include: (a) readiness for change, (b) trust-to-doubt, and (c) collective efficacy. In order for a public school to experience a transformation, the culture of the school must focus on the needs of the learners and align the adults to those needs. Schooling must empower learners to be ready and proficient for the twenty-first century. Staff members must realize and be ready for change, they must feel safe to doubt current practices, and feel that together they have the efficacy to make this a reality for their learners in their school.

3. Public education must become an institution that builds capacity in principals, teachers, and learners to partner to achieve *proficiency for all*. Using the revised Learner Improvement Cycle as a vehicle with the professional judgment of the teacher, the focus is now on the learning and the learner. In this cycle the assessing, evaluating results, and planning all should be a joint responsibility with the learner. The learning, the fourth step in the cycle, is a process more managed by learners who will need to know how to be self-learners (self-starter, autonomous) in the twenty-first century. This learning can come from resources, peers, or adults.

4. Improved practice and sustainability, using a continuous improvement cycle, must support a system that ensures *proficiency for all*. Continuous improvement plays out in several ways. Within each continuum there is a PCDA step to assist adults in their planning within a PLC, based on the input from the learners. This provides a systemic and consistent method for the stakeholders to address issues as they arise.

In a learner-centric, standards-driven classroom, the learners are actively involved in the continuous improvement of their learning and their communication with each other and the teacher. Within the Learner Improvement Cycle, there is a feedback loop between the learners, peers, and the teacher to refine the approaches to evidence proficiency on the standards. Improvement of the learning environment can be accomplished through the use of tools and processes to elicit learners' true voice and feedback.

Our learners' results have sounded an alarm in our educational system! Our country needs to get the best educational researchers and practitioners in a summit to discuss how public education will be reinvented to include the learner.

The Secretary of Education should convene a National Summit, with experts from every aspect of education coming together with practitioners, to make recommendations to reinvent a public-school system with emphasis on *proficiency for all*, twenty-first-century skill acquisition through involving the learner in their own learning. Next, challenge courageous school leaders to implement the recommended changes and provide continuous improvement support to ensure the new system meets the *proficiency for all* vision.

This brings a strategy to President Obama's vision of "hope" for every learner in our country. In his September 8, 2009, speech to American students, President Obama reinforced the authors' premise that students must support the efforts of the parents, teachers, and government to develop their twenty-first-century talents and skills. He challenged students to "take responsibility for their lives, for their education and set goals for themselves" (para. 29). He acknowledged that "being successful is hard . . . and you won't necessarily succeed at everything the first time you try" (para. 33). He concluded that "the story of America is about not people who quit when things got tough. It's about people who kept going, tried harder, who loved their country too much to do anything than their best" (para. 39).

The nation's governors recommended national standards in December 2009. As of July 2011, forty-four states have signed on to align their state's standards to the National Common Core standards. To compete in a global economy, this may be a step in the right direction; however, if the school systems that use these new national standards don't change the way they engage learners in the classroom, then this will be another instance of "hitting the snooze button" and will have minimal impact on creating the transformation necessary in public education.

Secretary of Education Arne Duncan has proposed everyone have an extended school day and year, and while this may be well-intended, if our nation's schools continue with the same current-level of archaic practices, giving learners more of the same will not lead to improved achievement. Learners must be leveraged in their own education and given the time and resources that they need to support this second-order change in our country.

The authors agree with Marvin Haberman (1991), that changing education isn't just important, but is a matter of life and death. What have we done since he said this?

Key Point of Reawakening the Learner:

How will *you* create a transformation in our schools to ensure *proficiency for all* learners to meet the ever-changing needs in the twenty-first century?

References

Ainsworth, L. (2003). *Power standards: Identifying the standards that matter the most.* Englewood, CO: Advanced Learning Press.

American Diploma Project. (2004). *"Ready or not": Creating a high school diploma that counts.* Washington, DC: Achieve, Inc.

American Psychological Association. Center for Psychology in Schools and Education. (1997). *Learner-centered psychological principles: A framework for school reform and redesign.* November. www.apa.org.

American Society for Quality. (2004). *Plan-Do-Check-Act Cycle.* www.asq.org/learn-about-quality/project-planning-tools/overview/pdca-cycle.html.

Arizona Community Foundation. (2008). *Educating Arizona.* January. Phoenix, AZ: Arizona Community Foundation.

Bandura, A. (1997). *Self-efficacy: The exercise of control.* New York: Freeman.

Bridges, W. (2003). *Managing transitions: Making the most of change.* 2nd ed. Cambridge, MA: Da Capo Press.

Brinson, D., and Steiner, L. (2007). *Building collective efficacy: How leaders inspire teachers to achieve.* The Center for Comprehensive School Reform and Improvement Issue Brief. October. www.centerforcsri.org.

Bryk, A. S., and Schneider, B. (2002). *Trust in schools: A core resource for improvement.* New York: Russell Sage Foundation.

Centennial BOCES. (1997). *Becoming a standards-based school/system.* Goals 2000 Grant. *Change readiness questionnaire.* www.scribd.com/doc3099867/Change-Readiness-Questionnaire.

Clarke, S. (2008). *Active learning through formative assessment.* London: Hodder Education.

Colorado Consortium for Data-driven Dialogue. (2004). *Preparing Tomorrow's Teachers to use Data (PTD) Project.* www.ptd-co.org/ppts/PTD_Overview.ppt.

Cornelius III, E. T. (2007). *Leading a "readiness for change" culture.* www.collegiateproject.com.

Darling-Hammond, L., Ancess, J., and Falk, B. (1995). *Authentic assessment in action: Studies of schools and students at work.* New York: Teacher's College.

Delorenzo, R., Battino, W., Schreiber, R., and Carrio, B. G. (2009). *Delivering on the promise.* Bloomington, IN: Solution Tree.

DuFour, R., and Eaker, R. (1998). *Professional learning communities at work: Best practices for enhancing student achievement.* Alexandria, VA: Association for Supervision and Curriculum Development.

DuFour, R., DuFour R., Eaker, R., and Karhanek, G. (2004). *Whatever it takes*. Bloomington, IN: Solution Tree.

DuFour, R., Eaker. R., and DuFour, R. (2005). *On common ground*. Bloomington, IN: Solution Tree.

Eaker, R., DuFour, R., and Burnette, R. (2002). *Getting started reculturing schools to become professional learning communities*. Bloomington, IN: National Education Service.

Fisher, D., and Frey, N. (2008). *Better learning through structured teaching*. Alexandria, VA: Association for Supervision and Development.

Fullan, M. (2001). *Leading in a culture of change*. San Francisco: Jossey-Bass.

———. (2005). *Leadership and sustainability*. Thousand Oaks, CA: Corwin Press.

Gladwell, M. (2002). *The tipping point: How little things can make a big difference*. New York: Back Bay Books.

Goddard, R. D. (2003). The impact of schools on teacher beliefs, influence, and student achievement: The role of collective efficacy beliefs. In J. Raths and A. C. McAninch, eds., *The Beliefs and Classroom Performance: The Impact of Teacher Education*, 183–202. Greenwich, CT: Information Age Publishing.

Goddard, R. D., Hoy, W. K., and Hoy, A. W. (2004). Collective efficacy beliefs: Theoretical development, empirical evidence and future directions. *Educational Researcher* 33 (3): 3–13.

Haberman, M. (1991). The pedagogy of poverty versus good teaching. *Phi Delta Kappan* (December): 290–94.

Hamm, M., and Adams, D. (2002). Collaborative inquiry: Working toward shared goals. *Kappa Delta Pi Record* 38 (3): 115–18.

Hoy, W. K. (2009). Collective efficacy scale. www.waynehoy.com/collective_efficacy.html.

Hoy, W. K., Smith, P. A., and Sweetland, S. R. (2002). A test of a model school achievement in rural schools: The significance of collective efficacy. In Wayne K. Hoy and Cecil Miskel, eds., *Theory and Research in Educational Administration*, 185–202. New York: McGraw-Hill.

Huba, M. E., and Freed, J. (2000). Learner-centered assessment on college campuses: Shift the focus from teaching to learning. Upper Saddle River, NJ: Pearson.

Kohm, B., and Nance, B. (2007). *Principals who learn: Asking the right questions, seeking the best solutions*. Alexandria, VA: Association for Supervision and Curriculum Development.

Kotter, J. (1996). *Leading change*. Boston: Harvard Business School Press.

Kouzes, J., and Posner, B. (2006). *A leader's legacy*. San Francisco: Jossey Bass.

Lambert, L. (1998). *Building leadership capacity in schools*. Alexandria, VA: Association for Supervision and Curriculum Development.

Lezotte, L. W. (1997). *Learning for all*. Okemos, MI: Effective Schools Products, Ltd.

Love, N., Stiles, K., Mundry, S., and DiRanna, K. (2008). The data coach's guide to improving learning for all students. Thousand Oaks, CA: Corwin Press.

Marzano, R. J. (2003). *What works in schools*. Alexandria, VA: Association for Supervision and Curriculum Development.

———. (2006). *Classroom assessment and grading that work*. Alexandria, VA: Association for Supervision and Curriculum Development.

———. (2007). *The art and science of teaching*. Alexandria, VA: Association for Supervision and Curriculum Development.

Marzano, R. J., and Kendall, J. S. (2008). *Designing and assessing educational objectives*. Thousand Oaks, CA: Corwin Press.

Marzano, R. J., Waters, T., and McNulty, B. A. (2005). *School leadership that works: From research to results*. Alexandria, VA: Association for Supervision and Curriculum Development.

MET Project. (2010). *Learning about teaching: Initial findings from the Measures of Effective Teaching Project*. MET Project research paper. Bill and Melinda Gates Foundation. www.metproject.org.

Meyer, J. (2009). Fed schools chief says kids need more class time. *Denver Post*, April 7. www .denverpost.com.

Novick, B., Kress, J. S., and Elias, M. J. (2002). *Building learning communities with character*. Alexandria, VA: Association for Supervision and Curriculum Development.

Obama, B. (2009). *Remarks by the president in a national address to America's schoolchildren*. [Transcription of television broadcast]. September 8. www.whitehouse.gov/the_press_office/ Remarks-by-the-President-in-a-National-Address-to-Americas-Schoolchildren.

Ormrod, J. (2004). *Human learning*. Upper Saddle River, NJ: Pearson.

Owen, R. C. (1999). *The teaching and learning cycle: A key construct of The Learning Network*. www .rcowen.com.

PL 107-110, The No Child Left Behind Act of 2001. www.ed.gov/policy/elsec/legislation/esea02/ index.html.

Partnership for the 21st Century. (2008). www.21stcenturyskills.org.

Perelman, S. J. (2009). thinkexist.com/quotes/s._j._perelman/.

Pink, D. H. (2006). *A whole new mind. Why right-brainers will rule the future*. New York: Berkeley Publishing Company.

Popham, W. J. (2008). *Transformative assessment*. Alexandria, VA: Association for Supervision and Curriculum Development.

Reeves, D. (2002). *The leader's guide to standards*. San Francisco: Jossey-Bass.

———. (2006). *The learning leader*. Alexandria VA: Association for Supervision and Curriculum Development.

Reh, F. J. (n.d.) *Managing change: Managing people's fear*. management.about.com/cs/people/a/ MngChng/092302.htm.

Rolheiser, C., and Ross, J. A. (1998). Student self-evaluation: What research says and what practice shows. www.cdl.org/resource-library/articles/self_eval.php?type=subject&id=4.

Sadker, M., and Sadker, D. (2004). *Teacher, schools, and society*. 7th ed. New York: McGraw-Hill.

Sass, E. (2008). *American educational history: A Hypertext timeline*. www.cloudnet.com/~edrbsass/ educationhistorytimeline.html.

SB 08-212. (2008). *Senate Bill 08-212: Colorado Achievement Plan for Kids. Summary and timeline— May 2008*. www.coloradoea.org/media/cap4k%20timeline%20final.pdf.

Schechter, C. (2006). Doubting schoolwork: Exploring an emerging concept. *Teachers College Record* 108 (12): 2474–96.

Schmoker, M. (2006). *Results now*. Alexandria, VA: Association for Supervision and Curriculum Development.

Senge, P. (1990). *The 5th discipline*. New York: Doubleday.

Sergiovanni, T. J. (2001). *Leadership: What's in it for schools?* New York: Routledge.

Shaun, K. (n.d.) *Achieve goal setting success with SMARTer goals*. www.selfgrowth .com/articles/ achieve_goal_setting_success.html.

Spady, W. G. (1994). *Outcome-based education: Critical issues and answers*. Arlington, VA: American Association of School Administrators.

Stanley, W., Smith, B. O., and Benne, K. (1943). Progressive essentialism. The *Teachers College Record* 9 (77): 209–13.

Stiggins, R. (2008). *Assessment manifesto: A call for the development of balanced assessment systems*. Portland, OR: ETS Assessment Training Institute.

Stiggins, R. J., Arter, J. A., Chappuis, J., and Chappuis, S. (2007). *Classroom assessment for student learning*. Upper Saddle River, NJ: Pearson.

Tomlinson, C. (2000). *Leadership for differentiating schools and classrooms*. Alexandria, VA: Association for Supervision and Curriculum Development.

Wiggins, G., and McTighe, J. (2005). *Understanding by design.* 2nd ed. expanded. Alexandria, VA: Association for Supervision and Curriculum Development.

Willis, G.B. (1999). *Cognitive interviewing: A "how to" guide.* Paper presented at the 1999 meeting of the American Statistical Association. appliedresearch.cancer.gov/areas/cognitive/interview/pdf.

Woolfolk, A. (2008). Student, teacher, and school collective efficacy. media.personcmg.com/ab/ab_podcasts_2/Efficacy.mp3.

York-Barr, J., Sommers, W. A., Ghere, G. S., and Montie, J. (2001). *Reflective practice to improve schools: An action guide for educators.* Thousand Oaks, CA: Corwin.

About the Authors

Copper Stoll has facilitated students' learning as a teacher, principal, and Chief Academic Officer in public schools for thirty years across America. She is currently an educational reformer in learner-centered practices with Gene in Don't Ever Stop, LLC and is an associate with other educational consulting firms.

Gene Giddings has served thirty-two years in American public schools as a teacher and principal. He is currently an educational consultant and co-partner with Copper in Don't Ever Stop, LLC and other educational reform businesses. You can contact Copper and Gene at donteverstopllc@gmail.com.